BEDSIDE GOLF

Peter Alliss
BEDSIDE GOLF

Illustrations by Bill Tidy

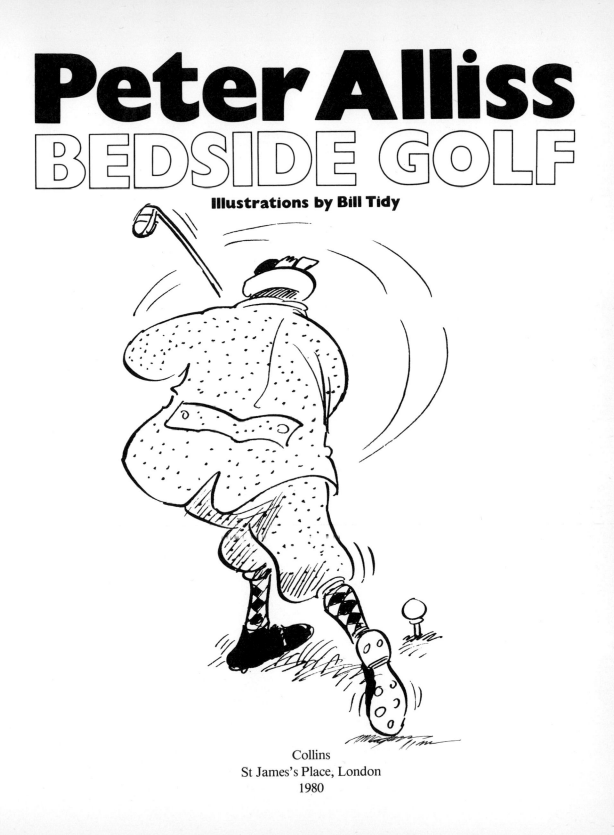

Collins
St James's Place, London
1980

First published in Great Britain 1980
by William Collins Sons and Co Ltd
London Glasgow Sydney Auckland
Toronto Johannesburg

Copyright © Peter Alliss 1980

ISBN 0 00 216293 8 HARDBACK
ISBN 0 00 216362 4 PAPERBACK

Made by Lennard Books
31 Bedford Row
London WC1R 4HE

Editor Michael Leitch
Art Director David Pocknell
Designer Michael Cavers
Photograph back cover: Peter Dazeley
Production Reynolds Clark Associates Ltd

Printed and bound in Spain by
Novograph, S. A., Madrid
Depósito Legal: M-4306-1981

Contents

The Game of Golf

t's a silly game. All games are silly, I suppose, but golf, if you look at it dispassionately, does go to extremes.

Players have to cover a huge area on the ground to carry out something that is really a very pedestrian exercise. And yet the drama and the excitement that golf generates, the sadness and the elation, are there *all* the time.

Other games have their dramas, of course. But usually those moments are over so quickly. If you take tennis, for instance, it's all wham, bang, ooh, ah, smash, in the net – and it's gone. Whereas if you're watching someone coming down the last hole of a great championship, the suspense can just build and build. The chap paces up and down, gets distracted and walks round and about again. All the while the tension grows. It doesn't matter how long he takes, there has to be a moment when he must draw back his club and hit the thing. Sometimes the slowness of it is the essence. You may feel like saying: come on, *do* something. But the game has got you, as well as him, in its grip.

I remember Doug Sanders in the Open Championship at St Andrews in 1970. He was in the classic situation. All he had to do was knock the ball in from just under

Trevino, to an opponent who has just putted five feet past the hole:
   'You wanna go and hit that now, while you're still mad?'

6

three feet. That was all he had to do. But suddenly he couldn't do it. He stood over the ball for a long time. Then he bent down to pick up something, a few blades of grass perhaps. Then he stood up and started again. His right shoulder moved forward, and the ball dribbled off to the right of the hole. His great chance was gone. He was forced to play-off with Nicklaus, who beat him.

To me that miss was one of the saddest moments in sport – comparable with Devon Loch collapsing 50 yards from the winning post in the Grand National when it was way ahead of the field; or with Neil Fox in the Rugby League Final missing the match-winning penalty from right under the posts in the last minute.

Since the early days of this century, people have been philosophizing about golf. J H Taylor, who with James Braid and Harry Vardon was one of the great triumvirate of golf in the 1900s, once said:

'Golf to the man or woman who regards it simply as a game will remain forever insoluble and an enigma: and it will retain its greatness because it contains something which lifts it higher than that of a mere pastime. Golf is more exacting than racing, cards, speculation or matrimony. Golf gives no margin, either you win or you fail. You cannot hedge, you cannot bluff, you cannot give a stop order, you cannot jilt. One chance is given you and you hit or miss. There is nothing more rigid in life and it is this extreme rigidity which makes golf so intensely interesting.'

Taylor touches on another interesting aspect here, which is the honesty that the game demands of its players. There is a story to illustrate this which concerns the great Bobby Jones. He was away in the rough, where no one could see him, and moved the ball in error while lining up his shot. When he came back at the end of his round he declared a penalty stroke, and was astonished when a couple of people suggested to him that it didn't really matter: if no one had seen him do it, what difference did it make? Jones looked at them as if they were potty. How could he not have declared it – that was Jones's view. To play the game any other way was unthinkable. In the end, the only person you would be fooling would be…yourself.

Perhaps Bobby Jones's devilish advocates were under the spell of one of the impressive list of golf-induced ailments isolated by Dr A S Lamb, of McGill University, when he wrote:

'Golf, it is said, increases the blood pressure, ruins the disposition, spoils the digestion, induces neurasthenia, hurts the eyes, blisters the hands, ties kinks in the nervous system, debauches the morals, drives men to drink or homicide, breaks up the family, turns the ductless glands into internal warts, corrodes the pneumogastric nerve, breaks off the edges of the vertebrae, induces spinal meningitis and progressive mendacity, and starts angina pectoris.'

Sir Walter Simpson apparently thought that the game of golf didn't screw people up quite so severely. He was more struck by the universal appeal of the game and, many moons ago, wrote this about it:

'Golf is a game for the many. It suits all sorts and conditions of men. The strong and the weak, the fit and the maimed, the octogenarian and the boy, the rich and the poor, the clergyman and the infidel. The late riser can play comfortably and be back for his rubber of bridge in the afternoon, the sanguine man can measure himself against those who will beat him, the half-crown seeker can find victims, the gambler can bet, the man of high principle may play for nothing and yet feel good. You can brag and lose matches, deprecate yourself and win them. Unlike the other Scotch game of whisky drinking, excess in it is not injurious to the health.'

In a more gentle vein is David Forgan's description, below. He was a skilled calligrapher, and used to produce charming panels in the style of illuminated addresses. In one he wrote:

'Golf is a science, the study of a lifetime in which you can exhaust yourself but never your subject. It is a contest, a duel or a mêlée calling for courage, skill, strategy and self-control. It is a test of temper, a trial of honour, a revealer of character. It affords a chance to play the man and act the gentleman. It means going into God's out-of-doors, getting close to nature, fresh air and exercise, a sweeping of mental cobwebs and a genuine relaxation of tired tissues. It is a cure for care, an antedote for worry. It offers companionship with friends, social intercourse, opportunities for courtesy and kindliness, and for generosity to an opponent. It promotes not only the physical health but moral force.'

do not think there is a much better way of following golf than on television. True, you miss the involvement and the atmosphere of being at an event, but television allows you to see far more than you would ever be able to follow as a spectator on the course.

At the British Open Championship, for instance, we start at 10.45 in the morning and go through until 7 o'clock, and then show the highlights later in the evening. This blanket coverage might seem idyllic, but there is apparently an unwritten law which says that the more golf you show people, the more complaints you get. 'Why didn't you show so-and-so?' 'I wanted to see the other match.' 'Listen, you stayed with him for 10 minutes and then you switched to *him*.' And so it goes on.

The problem at our end is to keep the interest going. This is especially true in head-to-head matches, when one player is clearly winning and there isn't really enough good material to fill the time allotted. That's when one gets the urgent voice in the ear:

'Can you think of something to give it a bit of a lift?' says the voice.

Inwards groans from the commentator. In America it's more difficult. Audiences are more fickle, and switch from one channel to another when they think something more exciting is going to happen on the other side. And, because TV people are so ratings-conscious, there's always that extra pressure to hang on to the viewers for as long as you can. So, if you've got a rather flat match, where the viewer thinks he knows who's going to win, you sometimes find yourself casting around desperately, even thinking, well, God forbid, but if only he'd fall down a hole, or be bitten by a dog, we'd be all right!

Panic can also strike with identifications. You're looking at your monitor when the producer cuts to a new hole – and suddenly the players aren't the ones you were expecting. The two you thought would show up have been delayed – perhaps one of them lost a ball – and have been supplanted by two men you've never seen before. Panic. Who the hell are they? Perhaps it's Smith and Brown. According to the programme they would be next. The voice in the ear hisses that it thinks one of them is Smith. It's the only golf they've got at the moment. Do you know anything about them? No. Oh, God. Let's assume it is Smith and Brown. What does it say in the programme? Name and club. Anything else? No. Probably a couple of little-known young professionals who just managed to quality. Gloom all round. Seconds have passed. Speak. You must speak. In finely modulated, confident tones you say:

'Interesting match coming up now. Here's young Smith from Blackburn. Very promising young player.'

It's not much. But it's the best you can do, hunched before the monitor in the BBC's 'Potting Shed', as I am inclined to call our commentary box. This architectural wonder, which the Americans find hilarious, is a 'studio', usually about 16 to 18 feet long. The builders install a shelf and set three or four TV monitors on them at an angle. Harry Carpenter has one, I have another or share one with Clive Clark, Alex

Hay or Mark McCormack – our other major voices! In the middle sits a scorer who keeps a check on what's happening out on the course.

Harry Carpenter always looks immaculate, at least, the part of him that you see at home. Around his feet are mounds of cable and all kinds of strange gear.

FALLING DOWN A HOLE THAT BIG ISN'T GOING TO HELP THE RATINGS!

It's rather like a theatre, except that backstage and onstage are in the same place, kept apart by a fine dividing line that runs through Harry Carpenter's waist. It might be amusing one day to show people the apparent chaos that really reigns in our 'little Potting Shed'.

The Americans isolate it very well. When I go over there now I have my own individual trailer, with a desk and two television sets. One is in black and white and gives a continual update of the scores, and the other shows the programme that is being broadcast, with any slow-motion shots. With those, a pad and pen, a jug of water and some sandwiches, I'm well prepared and peaceful. It's not at all like the hectic Potting Shed, where you can get three or four voices in your ear instead of the single voice of the producer telling you what's going on. Having said that, I still very much enjoy the British system because you can hear what the others are saying on air and you can avoid repetition. It's all rather confusing when you start out doing your first few commentaries, but in the end it's all worthwhile.

Since I *appear* to have such a remarkable grip on it all, you might therefore think my commentaries deserve only the highest praise. But that is not always the case. As I mentioned earlier, you can't hope to please all viewers everywhere. People have their favourite players and think we should show only them. Others deeply resent any form of autobiographical intrusion. If I have a cold, I had better not draw attention to it – as if it wasn't already obvious – and certainly not apologize for it. If I do, this is the response:

Dear Alliss,
Yesterday I had to write complaining about one
commentator being boring about his brother in
New Zealand. Now we have you babbling on
about your cold. What on earth makes you think
any of us are interested in your cold? Who do you
think you are – the most popular boy in the dorm?
I wish you commentators would realize that most
of your dribble, dribble is unnecessary and
unwanted.

That was at the British Open in 1979. The same cold drew further sympathy
from Penzance:

Dear Mr Alliss,
I see nothing to be proud of in the fact that you
have passed on your cold to everybody else. Had
you not been so mean you would have stayed at
home and kept your damned cold to yourself. It
did nothing to improve the quality of your
commentary.

After Lord Scanlon played in the Pro-Celebrity series, I received a fierce
broadside from a lady who shall be nameless:

Dear Mr Alliss,
Please don't spoil the enjoyment of golf with half-
baked discussions on trade unions. We get quite
enough of that on other programmes. I felt really
cheated tonight when, having given up another
programme to watch you, I found myself tuned in
to yet another party political broadcast.
        Stick to your knitting and talk to your
guests about golf, their problems or experiences
with the game. And please, when you are covering
a big tournament, could you give us a few more
details about the distances, choice of club, and
what the player is hoping to achieve. We don't
need to be told it was 'a beauty'. Tell us how and
why.

I say. I wonder who rattled her cage on the morning of 20 June 1979. On the
other hand, if that was a cloud, here's a bit of silver lining. From Barnton Avenue,
Edinburgh, came this somewhat more palatable message:

Peter Alliss,
I've just watched you and Lord Hugh Scanlon on
BBC 2. Quite marvellous. Keep it up. There are
always two sides to a story. My old man and I had
a game with you and your father many years ago
at Ferndown. He went round in 72. A few days
later we played again with you and you had a 72.
You couldn't putt, though. Your father could.

**Eleanor Ness,
Edinburgh.**

Now here's a very interesting piece of golfing history which might well have
remained unknown to the world at large had it not been for the medium of television.

Dear Peter,
At St Andrews last week you mentioned Bobby
Locke's famous hickory-shafted putter. I think
you may be interested in some of the history of
that club. At the turn of the century an aunt of
mine, then Miss Annie Dennison, later Mrs Jack
Graham, emigrated to South Africa, and apart
from becoming a South African lawn tennis
champion, she also played golf. Bobby Locke was
her caddy. And when she retired from golf she
gave him her putter, which he fancied. And that
was the one with which he had such success in his
heyday.

**J C P Dennison,
Chipping Campden,
Gloucestershire.**

Two rather more crisp letters caught my attention recently. Both revealed a
fairly frantic concern with the amount of time on TV that is devoted purely to golf.

Dear Sirs,
I would like to know why your fine commentary
of the British Open Golf Championship from
Royal Lytham & St Anne's is continuously
interrupted by cricket. I consider it a gross insult
from the British Broadcasting Corporation to
broadcast a homosexual sport which only caters
for the bum-boys of England and Wales. Britons
north of the border generally are not entertained
by a bunch of Anglo-Saxon poufs chasing each
other about a field. As far as I am concerned the
Fairy to blame can take his cricket and stuff it
right up...*

Watlow Avenue, Glasgow.

*The letter here goes into anatomical detail which I felt we might spare our more tender readers. The vehemence of the writer's passion for golf is something I find peculiarly Scottish.

On a Pro-Celebrity programme Glen Campbell was telling the story of a man who was a tennis nut. He had a beautiful new girlfriend, and one day he got so involved with a tennis match that he was nearly late for his date. He just had time for a quick shower, then he stuffed two tennis balls in his pockets and hared off to meet his girl. They had a nice candle-lit dinner and got up to dance to a slow smoochy tune, and the tennis balls pressed against the girl.

'What's that?' she asked.

'That's my tennis ball.'

'Oh, is that something like tennis elbow?'

This provoked an enraged letter from a viewer in St Andrews, who informed me that Glen's joke should have been edited out, that I should stand condemned, that he was not interested in whether I read *Playboy* or not, that he wished to watch golf and not filth, that my comments were normally puerile, that he frequently turned the sound down before the programme came on, etc, etc.

I really ought to put him in touch with my other fan, the anti-cricket viewer from Glasgow. Hell hath no fury like a Scotsman who thinks he is being deprived of his golf!

Members' Rights

ne thing that has always intrigued me is that in Britain people don't wish to pay anything to be a member of a golf club. If, for instance, the subscriptions go up to £150 a year, which is roughly £3 a week, which is less (far less in most cases) than a round of drinks, people are quite horrified.

'A hundred and fifty pounds! God help us,' they say.

In their anguish they forget that the average price of a green fee nowadays is £5. So it would cost them £250 or £300 a year if they played once a week as a non-member at a fairly modest club.

You might think, therefore, that £150 a year was pretty good value to be a fully fledged member of a golf club. But not the British. For that money they expect a few other things as well. They take for granted a beautifully groomed golf course. They also want a proper car park – all tarmacadamed with no lumps, bumps or holes. They want a superb men's locker room with carpeted floors – they've gone beyond the stage of tolerating the old miner's conveyor-belt stuff that used to be put on the floor. They want a proper drying room which isn't full of decaying gardening clothes, all ponging like hell. And they want a steward who, no matter how much they insult him, will always come back smiling and nodding, ready for more punishment. Then there's the card school on Friday night. If they wish to stay until 2 or 3 am, the steward will always say:

'You're more than welcome to stay, gentlemen. And of course we'll make you ham sandwiches, tongue sandwiches, and of course Mr Jackson, I know you don't like tongue so I've kept some tinned salmon for you, and I know you all like the sardine and cucumber sandwiches, and that you'll be wanting them served, some with the crusts off and some with the crusts on, at 2.30 am.'

This all duly happens, and two pound notes are pressed into the steward's hand when the members leave, shortly before dawn.

The members also expect their subscription to include the use of a

Trevino, on bending his putt round the hole:
'Did I tell you I ate a banana this morning?'

NO...IT WASN'T MY BANANA!

billiard table, which should be beautifully brushed and the rest of the equipment spotlessly maintained.

They should be able to get a drink 24 hours a day, or at least from 8.30 in the morning until, certainly, 12 o'clock at night. Golf clubs that operate the pub-hour system are looked on with loathing.

'What do you mean,' they bellow, incredulous, 'you don't open the bar until 10.30? And close at 2.30? And then you don't open again until 5? And shut at 10? God, what's the place coming to?'

Then they want a super barmaid, or steward's wife, whom they covet. She must look like a blend of Elizabeth Taylor and Brigitte Bardot and wear the most sensuous clothes but not offend the lady members. She also must not offend the male members, and she must on no account give the club captain a cardiac arrest.

That, briefly, is the required combination *inside* the clubhouse. Outside, there's the professional. He's an accountant, a psychologist and a psychiatrist. He has got to be as good an after-dinner speaker as Clement Freud. He has got to be a John Jacobs at giving lessons. He has got to be able to play golf as well as Arnold Palmer and Jack Nicklaus combined. He should have a marvellously stocked shop with about £300,000 worth of goods in it. He should be prepared to give enormous discounts. He should be prepared to take in clubs – trade-ins – at the whim of any of the members, and they must be allowed to make all such deals on their own terms. He should always be prepared to give away golf tees on the basis that it is a bit *infra dig.* to charge for such trivia. He should put himself out to teach all the younger members, and give all the members' young children lessons for nothing.

He should not appear in a new car too often – if in a car at all. That is a finely balanced matter, however, because if he appears to be doing well and he comes in on a push-bike, that can be thought to be overdoing it a bit, and he risks being accused of inverted snobbery. It is all right to have a Ford 2-litre, but if he moves into the 2.3-litre class, or higher, or gets an estate car, or one with a sunshine roof, then people will think he is doing too well, and letters may be written to the committee suggesting that he is charging too much for lessons.

In the summer he's got to be prepared to put in at least 100 hours a week. Especially in places north of St Albans, where people are said to work much harder than those that live south of St Albans, the members don't start arriving at the clubs until 6 o'clock in the evening. It stays light in the North until 10.30, and that's when play stops.

After that the professional has to run his club-cleaning and shoe-cleaning service. All clubs must be ready for play the next time the member needs them, perhaps three times a week in the warm months. The professional is permitted to charge extra for this service, and his rate has recently been upped to £10 a year, but it still doesn't actually cover the cost of the shoe polish.

In the summer the steward – bless him again – or his wife is also in extra demand. The committee suddenly decides:

'Wouldn't it be nice, after we've played, it's been such a good summer, why don't we, round about 10.30, why don't we put on something like bacon and egg, and sausage, and kidneys, mushrooms, fried bread, and beans, a big pot of tea or a pint of Tetleys? That would all go down very well, wouldn't it?' All concur.

Later the secretary gets in the steward and tells him of the new plans.

'Of course, steward, you've got all the catering rights, but I think you really ought to be able to do a thing like that for about 60 pence. We don't want to charge the members more than 60 pence.'

If the steward tries to point out that sausages cost x and beans y, and it's all going to cost rather more, he is likely to be addressed as follows:

'Look, um, steward, you've got a very nice job here. You've got a flat, you don't pay for any heat or light or other extras. Do you mean to say you can't do bacon, egg – er, two eggs – sausage, kidneys, mushrooms, fried bread, baked beans, a

pot of tea and perhaps two or three slices of bread and best butter, with the crusts on, for 60 pence? You can't? Well, you know, I think you had better start looking around. I'm not sure there's anything much more we can do for you here...'

And so the rigmarole goes on, from year to year. It certainly helps to explain why we don't have even one really super club in Britain. A real palace of golf. Of course, there *are* some clubs that are exclusive, for various reasons. But for the most part people are too busy straining in the opposite direction – to find that nice middle-of-the-road club that costs them as little as possible.

In my view this has had an unfortunate effect in that British clubs have become too much like each other. I personally wouldn't mind seeing a bit more extravagance here and there, a few Persian rugs on the floor, gold taps in the showers, delicious masseuse, that sort of thing. Surely I can't be the only one.

A Sort of Paradise

To harp a little further on the theme of creature comforts, the nearest thing to total luxury that I have seen was in the United States, at the Champions Club. This club was started outside Houston by two professional chums of mine, Jimmy Demaret and Jack Burke. Some 25 years ago they began buying scrub and swamp land at a place 40 miles or so from downtown Houston. Everyone thought they were mad, but they had done their homework and they knew that a big new highway was going to be built which would run past their land and put it within 35 or 40 minutes' drive from the centre of town.

They built two golf courses and the whole venture has been enormously successful, with a huge membership. The Ryder Cup match was played there in 1967. But what was so striking was the way Demaret and Burke went about getting the best of everything for their club. They picked out in their minds all the super things they had seen at all the clubs they'd been to.

They remembered, for instance, that Charlie was the best man in the shoe trade. He had always cleaned their shoes immaculately. But he was at the Baltimore Country Club, or wherever. So they went up there and persuaded Charlie to come and take charge of cleaning the shoes at their club. They set about getting their head barman and chef in the same way.

The clubhouse is basically in three units. In the middle is the bar and restaurant and an area where you can sit out. This is all open-plan and subdivided by plants and bushes. Then there's the men's locker room on one side and the women's on the other.

The men's locker room is extraordinary, a sort of paradise. It's a huge room that divides into alcoves containing the lockers and showers. In the centre there are 10 massive round tables each big enough for 10 people, with comfortable swivel armchairs and holders for the members' glasses.

The sanitary arrangements make one fantasize about the ultimate in golf clubs. The kind of place that would offer you three types of toilet paper – the brutal hard-and-shiny, the medium-gentle, and the pastel-shaded flakey-soft (needing at least 14 pieces for satisfactory results). Allied to all that are beautiful marble wash-basins and a great pageant of lotions and potions, hair creams and after-shave lotions, electric razors and safety razors, all laid out for the members' use. Beautiful combs stand by in tubes three-quarters filled with that special fluid which homogenizes, anaesthetizes and cleans everything. In the corners are piles of gigantic snow-white towels and bathrobes. There is one of those sophisticated weighing machines which always weighs three or four pounds light to make you feel better.

After your game of golf you could come in, have a shower, pamper yourself with a few lotions, then on with a great towelling bathrobe, and special club slippers, sit down at the table, order a drink and club sandwich then settle down to a game of poker or bridge for a couple of hours. Really, there would be no need for the members ever to leave the locker room except to play golf.

Even that has been taken care of. If you desire, there is a video machine now which uses a big wall screen, about 10 feet by 6 feet, on which golf holes are projected. The player stands up facing it and whacks a ball which is on a rubber arm, and his shot is registered on a computer which tells him how far his ball has gone and in which direction.

'Your ball has gone 210 yards and you are just off the fairway, in light rough,' it says. '140 yards to the green.'

You select your next club and whack the ball again. The computer goes click-click-click-click-click. Aah, bad luck, you've just gone into the sand. So you bang out of there with a sand-wedge. Now you're on the green. And there, i.e. in front of where you've been hitting this ball on a rubber arm, is a small patch of simulated grass with a regulation-sized golf hole in the middle. You putt, and your shot is gauged in feet by the machine. Yes, it's in. Well done. So then you mark your card.

The machine offers a selection of about 18 of the greatest golf courses in the world. You can play at Sunningdale, Cypress Point, Pebble Beach, Burning Tree, St Andrews, Turnberry, and so on. If you can do all that while still wrapped in the cossetting warmth of a magnificent clubhouse, why bother to go out and take a chance with the weather?

PARDON ME, SUH.
THIS IS THE LADIES TEE!

Heavenly Golf

Golf has always attracted a fair amount of attention from the Church. Christy O'Connor is often followed round by a small band of Irish Catholic priests in black shiny suits who chuckle mysteriously when Christy holes a difficult putt. I have never been quite sure whether they are invoking His help on Christy's behalf or just having a good outing.

There are some notable upholders of the clean religious life on the circuit, who more or less seem to expect that if they never entertain wicked thoughts, never read *Playboy,* etc., then Jesus will guide their putts into the hole. Henry Longhurst was sceptical about this whole business of calling on God to improve your game. On one occasion he pointed out to a rather over-earnest type that if he called on God he would in fact be cheating, since one of the rules of golf explicitly forbids the use of any outside agency!

But the likelihood that there *is* Someone up there has inspired many many responses from golfers. It explains, for example, the tactful reaction of our vicar at Ferndown who, whenever he hit a really bad shot, used to thunder at the top of his voice:

'BRASS-BOUND BUCKETS!!!' A most effective choice of words which, presumably, offended Nobody.

As to whether they do have golf courses in Heaven, I am not prepared to say, but certainly there have been a number of stories which develop that theme. One story concerns Jesus and St Peter, who used to play each other regularly. St Peter's only vice was that he used to spend all his spare cash on golf books, new equipment, putters, any new gimmick that came out, kangaroo-skin golf bags and the rest. He had the whole lot: plus-fours, plus-twos, tapered trousers, lambswool and cashmere sweaters...everything he could possibly need for hot weather, wet weather, cold weather.

Jesus, on the other hand, wasn't so bothered about his equipment. He had an old set of clubs that had been handed down from his father. He used to repaint his own golf balls. In his spare time he would mooch about the course looking for a few lost balls. Jesus used to play in sandals. In winter he'd dip his feet in Nev to make them tolerably waterproof and knocked some nails into the undersides of his sandals. These gave him a bit of grip, but compared with St Peter's crocodile shoes the sandals did look rather shabby.

19 th

One day they were on the first tee. A coin was spun, and St Peter won the toss. He'd been practising for about half an hour on the driving range and was feeling really loose. He put down a new Slazenger B-51, and after one or two preliminary waggles hit a beautiful drive right down the middle of the fairway, about 245 yards with just a touch of draw. From there he was in an ideal position for a medium iron shot up to the first green.

Jesus hadn't hit any practice balls and decided he would use a No. 3 wood off the first tee. He didn't want to risk his best ball because there was a lot of heather slightly downhill from the fairway. So, without even having a practice swing, he took a gi-normous swish at the ball. Jesus, in fact, did like to give the ball a bit of stick. It was his great delight to crack the ball as hard as he could.

On this occasion, though, Jesus was a bit unlucky in the hitting area. He only just caught the top of the ball and it went a mere 15 or 20 yards, coming to rest in thick heather.

The two players picked up their clubs and started walking. St Peter, of course, had a caddy to help him with his bag – a new water buffalo-skin monster that he was trying out for the first time. Jesus had one of the pencil variety.

Just about 10 feet or so from where they thought Jesus's ball had landed, a mole popped up its head. It walked over and took Jesus's ball between its little front feet, and started off through the heather. As soon as it got to the fairway an eagle, circling overhead, spotted the mole and thought, 'Ah, that looks a tasty dish,' swooped down and with its great talons took hold of the mole and flew off. The mole clung like grim death to the golf ball as the great eagle glided down the fairway.

As the eagle reached the green, the sky suddenly darkened and there was an enormous crack of thunder. This startled the eagle, which dropped the mole, which in turn dropped the ball and, would you believe, the ball landed on the putting surface and went trickle, trickle, trickle into the hole.

St Peter turned to Jesus and said:

'Are you going to muck about all day, or are we going to have a proper game of golf?'

THESE 'HOLES-IN-ONE' ARE COSTING HIM A BOMB!

A keen golfer went to Heaven, and was very surprised to find that they had the most beautiful golf course there. It was built on rather American lines with water hazards, tree-lined fairways, big bunkers, white sand...it really was a joy. The new arrival was being shown round by St Peter who, as we know, was a very keen golfer. They came to the 8th, which was a short hole of about 195 yards, and stopped to watch a couple up on the tee.

WATER HAZARD

The first player stood up and hit a No. 4 wood. He hit it well and it landed nicely on the putting surface. The second chap seemed to umm and ahh for a bit, then he took out an iron which looked very lofted. He gave the ball the most enormous whack but the ball didn't even reach halfway over a lake running across in front of the green. He took out another ball, and gave it a tremendous crash. In the water again. He did this five times, and on every occasion the ball landed in the water, 30 or 40 yards short of the green.

The new arrival in Heaven couldn't resist any further, and he turned to St Peter and said:

'Who on earth does he think he is? Jesus Christ?'

St Peter replied, 'Actually, that is Jesus Christ. The trouble is, he thinks he's Arnold Palmer.'

A very enthusiastic golfer had a friend who was a noted clairvoyant, and he was always badgering his friend to contact someone from the beyond to see whether there was a golf course in Heaven. If there was, he wanted to know what sort of sand was in the bunkers, which were the out-of-bounds holes, how difficult the course was, what was par, whether there was a grill room, a good pro's shop, and so on.

The clairvoyant eventually said that when he had his next seance he would make some inquiries. So he did that, and about three weeks later the keen golfer saw the clairvoyant and asked whether he had any news.

'Yes,' said the clairvoyant, 'I have some good news and some bad news. The good news is that there is the most superb golf course in Heaven. It's beautiful. It has Bermuda grass on the fairways and Penn Cross on the greens, the most beautiful crushed marble in the bunkers. There is a superb clubhouse with a grill room, a marvellous men's locker room, a splendid pro's shop, golf carts, etcetera. It is really tip top.'

'That's great,' said the golfer. 'But what's the bad news?'

'I booked you a starting time for next Tuesday at 2 o'clock.'

Lee's Last Word

I noticed once on our Pro-Celebrity series that Lee Trevino seemed to have the idea that it was possible to interfere with a golf ball while it was in flight. Lee's sense of the supernatural manifested itself to me after he had hit a tee shot and was standing there giving the ball rather a lot of verbal encouragement.

'Be up! Be up! Be up!' he kept calling.

But his caddy, Willie Aitchison, evidently disagreed because he was shouting:

'Come down! Come down! Come down!'

Lee could not stand competing for the attention of the gods, so he turned to Willie and ordered:

'Leave it alone Willie! Leave it alone!'

I wonder if that system *does* work.

The Feudal System

Things have changed a great deal since I was a lad. Many golf clubs are now democratic to a degree that would have been unthinkable before the war. I find, however, that not all the feudal customs have disappeared – and long may they remain, so far as I am concerned, because without them some clubs would be immeasurably poorer places.

To set the scene, as it used to be, here is one of those classic golfing jokes which for unbridled snobbery must take some beating.

All his life a dignified English lawyer, a widower with a considerable income, had dreamed of playing at Swinley Forest (or some other very private club). One day he had made up his mind to go along and chance it, although he was well aware that it was a very exclusive club and he might be turned away. When he asked if he might play on the famous course the secretary inquired:

'Are you a member?'

'No, I'm not.'

'Guest of a member?'

'No, Sir.'

'Sorry,' said the secretary, 'I'm afraid we have very strict rules here about this sort of thing.'

The lawyer was turning to leave when he saw a slightly familiar figure seated in the lounge reading *The Times*. It was Lord Wesley Parham. He approached and, bowing low, said:

'I beg your pardon, Your Lordship, but my name is Higginbottom of the London law firm of Higginbottom, Willerby and Barclay. I would like to ask you a huge favour. Do you think I could play on this delightful course as your guest?'

The Lord gave Higginbottom a long, cool look, put down his paper and asked:

'Church?'

'Episcopalian, and my late wife was Church of England.'

'Education?'

'Eton and Oxford. Double First.'

'Athletics?'

'Rugby, Sir, a spot of tennis, rowed number four against Cambridge.'

'Military?'
'Coldstream Guards, Sir. Brigadier. MC, DSO, wounded three times.'
'Campaigns?'
'Dunkirk, Alamein, Normandy, Sir.'
'Languages?'
'Fluent in French and German, just a touch of modern Greek.'
'Mmm,' said his Lordship. He gave the secretary a quick nod and said:
'I'll give you nine holes.'

WHERE ARE YOU OFF TO ? I MEANT
9 HOLES OF SNOOKER!

Classic Types

Today's golf club is socially broader than in days of old and seems to cater for the needs and desires of four basic types. First is the Club Bore. Usually retired, usually from one of the professions – either a dentist, doctor, lawyer, or from one of the armed services. He's been everywhere, done everything, and he spends his life at the club. He's always there by half-past nine or a quarter to ten, and poddles about between the bar and the golf course. Six holes here, two gins there, lunch, port, nine holes, gin, more gin.

Then there's the Young Jazzer. He derives from an earlier type, but has acquired more power which he seeks to use to dominate the older members. He is less hidebound than his archetype about dress, and has been heard to demand the freedom not to wear a jacket and tie. He is even prepared to go as far as a short-sleeved shirt.

The third type is the Miser. He wants to use all the facilities but not pay for anything, and is very strong on Members' Rights (see also page 16). He wants to be there all day long, takes magazines, papers, soap, tissues, anything from the locker room, but never subscribes to the staff fund at Christmas. He is always prepared to Make Do. (Sometimes he has to, anyway, because the club doesn't possess the particular facility, say a tennis court, that he wouldn't have minded using but which, thanks to his benighted predecessors, the club has failed to install.)

The final type is the Progressive Committee Man. He wants to graduate to become captain of the club and he wants to leave his Mark on Things. He may do this by getting on the Greens Committee, where he develops a near-obsession about the 10th hole.

'Wouldn't it be so much better if we moved the green 80 yards and put it up on that ledge where the big tree overhangs?' he asks at meeting after meeting until at last the desired change is agreed, and the first lines of his epitaph are written.

His next move is to become club captain. If he has money, and starts to splash it about, he is capable of frightening off the other members for years to come. The car park has been heavily potholed for years and suddenly he writes out a personal cheque and the job is done. Or the flagpole is getting a bit creaky, and he dishes out £1,500 for a new one. Or he insists, every time he enters the clubhouse, on buying a drink for everyone in sight.

This magnanimity can have a daunting effect on the other members. Anxiously they confer in corners.

'Taking it a bit far isn't he?'

'I should say so.'

'Hmm. Feel sorry for old Sid, taking over next year. Only works for the Electricity Board. Won't be able to keep up all this.'

Fortunately there are plenty of other ways for Sid and his successors to be good club captains without bombarding the establishment by cheque book. Golf club members, for all their shortcomings, are wise enough in the ways of the world to be suspicious of anyone who tries to buy popularity.

There is a story about the funeral of one of the most unpopular members of the club. He had been a member for donkey's years and put a lot of money into the club, but he was not liked because he behaved in such a boorish way and made life for everybody pretty miserable. When he died, people were amazed to see there was a colossal turn out at the funeral. One of the young committee members turned to the old secretary and said:

'I cannot believe it. This man was probably the most unpopular man in the club. Why on earth should all these people have turned up?'

The old wise secretary said, 'It just goes to show that if you give the people what they want, they will turn up.'

Dealing with Visitors

Visitors are tolerated provided they behave themselves. If they are foreigners, they may find this hard, and leave themselves open to some rather deft abuse. This was the fate of a party of loud American visitors at a usually rather exclusive club. They played a round and went into the clubhouse. They found neither showers nor baths in the locker room. They started yelling and shouting for the steward.

'Where the hell is the shower?'

The steward gave this marvellous reply:

'I am sorry gentlemen, but their Lordships usually repair back to their castles to bathe.'

Getting his Greens

In another classic tale of the golf club world a rather uncouth stranger arrived at a posh golf club. The club was going through rather rough financial times, so the man was able to talk his way onto the course, paying a green fee without an introduction by the secretary or any member of the club.

He looked a mess. He was wearing braces, his trousers were tucked into his socks, and on his feet he had a pair of battered grey plimsolls. He set off round the course and made a terrible botch of everything, stamping about in bunkers and not replacing his divots, leaving the flag out of the hole when he went on to the next tee, and generally behaving in a highly substandard fashion.

He eventually got back to the clubhouse, went in and sat down in the dining-room. He ordered a meal and was halfway through it when a rather military gentleman came up to him and tapped him on the shoulder.

'I say there. I'm Colonel Frederick Dawson, Greens Committee. I would like a word with you.'

At which the rather boorish chap looked up and replied:

'I want a word with you too, mate. Greens Committee. I'll tell you what, these brussels sprouts are bloody awful.'

THOSE BRUSSELS SPROUTS WERE DIVOTS!

The Road to Ruin

Nowadays golf professionals have *carte blanche* to go pretty well anywhere in the world and enter the portals of any great club. And quite often their caddies, their faithful Sancho Panzas, are right there with them. It was certainly very different in my father's playing days, and even in my own.

I remember very well how, in 1953, at the age of 22, I was on the verge of being picked for the Ryder Cup team. Word then percolated through that I *might* be afforded the facilities of the Ferndown Club, where my father had been the professional since 1939. But when the time approached to put it to the vote, a cautionary voice from the ranks of Colonel Blimps said:

'Should we not just wait and see whether he does in fact get into the Ryder Cup team?'

He no doubt felt that selection was going to make some enormous difference to my temperament and my personality – though quite how I've never been able to understand. Anyway, I did get into the team and I was allowed to use the clubhouse.

Having said that, I've always had the thought that more good men were ruined through being allowed into the clubhouse, and to participate in its activities than were ruined through being kept out. You may think that's being rather reactionary, and indeed it may well be, but I have seen it happen to too many golf professionals.

The trouble can often start in winter, when the cold weather seems to be going on for ever. There are always one or two members who are there every day, and it's not too long before one of them looks at the professional and says:

'Well. 10.30. Come on, we'll go and have a couple of Whisky Macs to get the old blood going.'

Then it would be:

'Come on, let's have a couple of frames of snooker.'

This would be followed by:

'Let's have a sandwich and then a couple of glasses of port.'

It is very easy for that sort of thing to become a very pleasant ritual, the more so if the snow's six inches on the ground. Then, of course, the job begins to suffer. In springtime the money that should have been put by to stock the shop has dwindled. Then the club gets irate, and the very men who participated in the 'downfall' of the professional are the first ones to throw up their hands in committee and declare:

'He's no good. Let's have him out.'

It's really up to each and every professional to do what he thinks best. But it's certainly not a disaster not to be asked into the clubhouse. Groucho Marx had a classic remark on the subject, which some may find consoling. He said:

'I don't care to join any club that's prepared to have me as a member.'

Getting In

The superb deviousness of Membership Sub-committees has been fictionally analysed by B E Gray of Harpenden, and I am grateful to him for sending me the following account:

We are very lucky at our golf club. The Membership Sub-committee, composed of senior businessmen well versed in the ways of the world, is not easily fooled. Since my election to the Committee last year I have watched its deliberations with deep interest and admiration.

Last week, after we'd elected the President's new son-in-law and the area manager of the club's bank, to which we were indebted for some £50,000, it was time to consider the nomination for the remaining vacancy.

'Cedric J Renfrew of The Willows, a chartered accountant with a present handicap of three,' intoned the Secretary.

'Well,' said the Captain, 'you've all met this young fellow. Seems a decent enough sort of chap. What do you think?'

'What does the J stand for?' asked Hemmings.

'I believe his second name is Jacob,' said the Secretary.

'Anything significant in that?' persisted Hemmings.

'I understand that his grandmother was connected by marriage to the Astor family, and that the use of the name is traditional and sentimental.'

'Good.'

'Well that's that then,' said the Captain. 'All in favour?'

'You know his wife's coloured, I suppose,' said Ramshawe, who had seconded the nomination.

'Good God! Coloured! Why weren't we told before?'

Ramshawe tried again. 'Well she's very charming and only partly coloured.'

'What do you mean, partly coloured? Which part?'

'Her parents are Eurasian.'

'You can't be much more coloured than that, can you?'

'What on earth was Jones doing, sponsoring an application without giving us the full facts?'

Ramshawe sighed deeply. 'I don't think Jones had much choice, really. You see, this Renfrew chap is a rather special sort of accountant, and he's given Jones a great deal of help.'

'What's his particular line of accountancy, then?'

'I don't really like to discuss this,' said Ramshawe. 'But it appears he's a wizard on tax avoidance schemes. Jones told me, in strict confidence of course, that he's already saved him £2,500 in just three months.'

'How very interesting. I must say, that rather puts things in a different light.'

'Yes, he seems a decent enough chap to me. You know, I think a sari would brighten up the club a bit.'

Ramshawe intervened. 'She doesn't wear a sari, actually. She's an MA and helps Renfrew with his work. Jones says they keep a very good sherry and their fees are most reasonable. Average is about 5 per cent of the nett tax saving.'

'Splendid.'

'Well,' said the Captain, 'let's not stay here all night.' He referred to the sheet in front of him. 'C J Renfrew, proposed by Jones, seconded by Ramshawe. All in favour? Good. Thank you, gentlemen. Next business.'

Caddies

magine that, a few years back, you have joined the crowd of spectators around a green just before the arrival of the players, one of whom is 1951 Open Champion Max Faulkner. Suddenly a wild-eyed figure, clad mainly in army surplus gear, detaches himself from the group round the players and marches across the green to where Faulkner's ball is lying. Round his neck a large pair of opera glasses hangs from a piece of thick string. You, by the way, are close enough to notice that there are no lenses in the glasses. Then, oblivious to all around him, this strange character flings himself on to the ground behind the ball and uses the opera glasses to line up the putt. Max comes up, and Opera-glasses appears to give him certain instructions. Now what would you have thought of that? Well, if you'd really wanted to know, you'd probably have needed only to ask the person next to you to be told:

'Oh, that's Mad Mac. Always caddies for Faulkner.'

Mad Mac was, admittedly, one of the more eccentric members of the breed – though there were others we shall meet in a minute. He was said to come from a well-to-do family, and had a brother who was an air commodore and another in the Foreign Office. True? I'm not sure. Anyway he was completely unselfconscious, and some of his activities were quite extraordinary.

One of Mad Mac's most treasured possessions was a battered old mashie, richly bound from neck to grip in layers of twine. He used to carry this club through the West End of London late at night, when there was not *too* much traffic about. He'd get to Piccadilly Circus, put a ball down near where Eros is – before they put all those awful railings around the place – and then just chip his way quietly down into Leicester Square.

Mad Mac's exploits had a certain style about them which you won't find so easily nowadays. But there were certain precedents in his day. In fact, it is one of golf's more hallowed sayings that there are three classes of people entitled to refer to themselves as 'We'. They are: kings, editors and caddies. With caddies, this preference for the first person plural must partly come from the extraordinary way they get wrapped up in the performance of 'their man'. It is marvellous to hear them telling stories about how well *they* were doing – until something went wrong that was entirely *his* fault. A caddy's version of events goes something like this:

'We were three under fours after 16, and then at 17 we 'it a great drive. It wasn't lying too well in the fairway so we played a 3 iron short of the cross-bunkers. This left a little punch shot up onto the green. We played to about 15 feet and then *he,* the bloody fool, three-putted.'

A more colourful tale in much the same vein has the old Aga Khan going to his caddy for a few tips. They went out for a few practice shots and the caddy was handling matters with his usual great diplomacy and patience.

'Keep your eye on the ball, Your Highness. Slowly back, Your Highness. Pause at the top, Your Majesty. Och, you've missed it again, you silly black bugger!'

Caddies used to have quite a reputation as wild men living on the fringes of

CALL THIS A GOOD TIME?

society, extravagant about racehorses while at the same time they were wearing the scruffiest clothes you ever saw – and which, often enough, they *had* slept in. Of course, things have changed enormously since those early days. Like most of us, they now arrive by car and stay in decent hotels – and that's good. With the growth of professional tournament golf and all the money involved, caddies are now earning something like £12 – £15 a day plus a bonus on winnings that can be as high as 5 per cent. If the golfer wins a really good purse, that can be a considerable amount of money.

Furley Davis

At Ferndown, where my father was the professional, we had a great man called Furley Davis. His family were big lace manufacturers in Nottingham, and his brother was a very well-known portrait painter. Furley was evidently the black sheep of the family. He was the caddy master at Ferndown.

My father discovered him in about 1939, when Furley was virtually sleeping rough under a hedge. He offered him a job and Furley installed himself in the caddies' shed, which was a modest brick building with some shelving at the back. Furley took out one of the shelves and put in a mattress, and that was his bed. From there he progressed in time to a larger garden shed.

Davis spoke three foreign languages, always smoked cigars, and used to do *The Times* crossword puzzle every day. Just after the war we used to get a few toffs down from London who'd stay at the Dormy Hotel. One of them was Victor Walker, an American who was the boss of Linotype. He used to like doing *The Times* crossword – and the *Telegraph* as well. Old Davis used to have *The Times* crossword done every day by quarter past nine. It's not many golf clubs that can boast that their caddy master had *The Times* crossword done by that time. So all these great men used to come down, and once they knew old Furley they used to go in and say:

'What's 3 Down, then, Davis?'

'Oh, it's so-and-so...anagram.'

'Oh, by God, yes, so it is.'

So there he was, this superb dropout, helping the high and mighty to finish off their crossword puzzles. He went on like that until well into the 1950s. He was 86 when he died.

He, in a way, was responsible for bringing the first golf trolleys into operation. These were the invention of a man called Tong, who ran a bicycle shop business in Bournemouth and who could have been the first in the world to come up with a golf trolley – although it's possible there may have been some in America before that.

What Tong did was to take a pair of the smallest bicycle wheels – 8 or 10 inches – and put a metal frame on them and a handle. You strapped your golf bag on it, pumped the tyres up, and away you went.

Tong took his invention along to my father and asked him if he wanted a share in it. My father said:

'That'll never do any good.'

And turned him down. In retrospect, it wasn't far short of turning down the Beatles. But at least my father did suggest to Tong that he should speak to the old caddy master about the idea. Well, he had a bit more business sense, picked up the idea and took about 20 trolleys on loan. He didn't make a fortune out of it because he had no way of patenting or marketing it. That was in the days of Austerity, when fortunes were hard to come by, especially if you had no capital. But the idea spread, and from that time golf club caddies began to dwindle.

YOU REALLY THINK I'D DO WELL IN THE TOUR DE FRANCE?

The Regulars

Today there are few clubs that have caddies. Another reason for the demise of the caddy is that boys in their early teens seem to have no desire to earn a few pounds pulling a trolley. That's not universally true, of course, but there really are very few clubs, except around London, where you can get a caddy. Sunningdale has some, and Wentworth, and Coombe Hill. And in Scotland the big clubs like Gleneagles have plenty for big occasions. But the great change has been in the professional tournaments, when the touring professionals started to take on their own caddies.

The 'regular caddy' was something that really began in the late '50s and early '60s. I had a lad called Jimmy Cousins. He was a Bournemouth boy and we worked together for about 11 years. He was perhaps the best-paid caddy on the tour. We used to start at the Sunningdale Foursomes, in the third week in March, and go through until the Gleneagles Foursomes in late October. He got a princely wage of £20 a week for that period. And if I had a bonanza year, which meant winning about £4,000, he got a 'present' or another few pounds.

How different nowadays, when caddies are on a good £80 a week and up to 5 per cent of winnings. It's hard to say how much they really contribute to the player to justify being on an overall percentage. It's like a boxer having someone in his corner who understands 'the game' and 'his' man. Certainly, there's nothing worse than having someone who annoys you, and if you're picking up casuals every week there's a big risk of that happening. In fact it's quite likely that he'll do the very thing that irritates you most in the first five minutes. But by then it's impossible to get anyone else, it's too late to train him and it's too late to say anything, and so you hubble and bubble inside and maybe take an 80.

Caddies of the old school are dying out. Things have become much more regulated, and we'll never see the old days again when people like Sheridan were about. He was the old caddymaster at Sunningdale and a remarkable character. His portrait hangs in the clubhouse. All that seems like another age, when people were allowed to look after their staff without everything being laid down in rules and regulations. Perhaps there were too many bad bosses in the old days, and the workers needed somebody to champion their cause. There's no doubt that a lot of people were well and truly sat on. But the whole thing's gone topsy-turvy now, it's hard to be a 'good boss' in the old sense and the classic caddy has disappeared.

The old caddy was a figure of wonder. Take Jaffa, who wore four overcoats summer and winter and wellington boots all slashed at the side to let his carbuncles out. He used to strip off once a year and dive into the canal by the golf club at Ealing and fish out several thousand golf balls.

Jaffa's carbuncles were the size of your fist and at the end of 36 holes on a hot day you could almost see the heat pulsating through the rubber of his wellingtons. A fearsome sight was Jaffa.

Then there was Canada. The first time I noticed him was in about 1960, when he was caddying for Harold Henning, the South African professional. He was a middle-aged man, with sandy hair, glasses, dignified. One evening I got into conversation with him and Harold and I asked him what he was going to do that night. He said:

'Oh, I'm working on my thesis on the Canadian Indians.'

He'd discovered that his grandparents had lived on the fringe of these Indians in Canada and he was writing up their history in his spare time. He had a great wodge

of papers on these Indians, going back some 250 years, which he kept in the back of an old A-30 he was running.

That was the first time I realized that all caddies weren't dropouts and heavy drinkers. But now there are three or four Americans who come over here to caddy. They tour the world, thanks to Freddy Laker's airline.

On the other hand, how about Angelo Argea, who caddies for Jack Nicklaus? He's even written a book about the caddy's life called *Jack and I.* And Dave Musgrove, who was with Ballesteros in his early years, he's done very well. Before they met up he'd done very little caddying but he took up with Ballesteros at just the right moment. The big-shot caddies had all got their runners, and no one really wanted to caddy for Ballesteros because he was still unknown. So it all turned out well for Mr Musgrove.

Tournament golf has become rather more scientific than it used to be. Players started to pace out the yardages, but nowadays in many cases it's the caddy's job to tell the player what the distance is to the hole. In the old days a caddy used to tell you which club to use and it was up to you to hit the ball right. Now, the caddy says:

'It's 185 yards to the front of the green, the pin's 18 yards on, so 203 yards total.'

So even if you are new to the course, your caddy will have got there the day before and walked it, and is in a position to give you the precise information you need to make your shot.

Of course, you want to make sure that you and your caddy speak the same language when it comes to measuring the distance in paces. If you take great long strides and he shuffles along with funny little steps, you could soon be in trouble. But once you've built up a basic trust, then that method can work very well.

Some caddies have become so closely identified with particular stars that they can be in enormous demand. There is a story, which I've heard attributed to more than one star and his caddy, but which has certainly been linked with Arnold Palmer.

IT'S EIGHTEEN YARDS TO THE APRON OF THE BAR... WATCH THE BARMAN AND THE BIG BLONDE... STICK TO GIN AND TONICS...

Tip's Tale

The story goes that a chap who could hit the ball a very long way indeed, and was very good, was determined to play Troon, the scene of Arnold Palmer's great victory in the Open championships. He managed to procure the services of Palmer's caddy, Tip Anderson, and insisted that Tip bring along all the notes and measurements for the course because he was going to play it in exactly the same way as Arnold Palmer, with precisely the same clubs and under the same weather conditions.

They had to wait a few days to get the ideal conditions, but eventually the day dawned, and they set off. After 10 holes he matched Palmer stroke for stroke, absolutely level, and he was delighted. He'd got the right clubs and the right line and it was all splendid. Then he got to the 11th, which at Troon is a very very difficult hole indeed – a par 4 with a slight dog-leg, gorse everywhere and the railway and wall hard against the green.

He hit the most super drive into the ideal position and turned to Tip and said:

'What did Palmer use here?'

'A 4 iron.'

He played a real fizzer right at the flag, but it stopped 50 yards short of the green. So he turned and said:

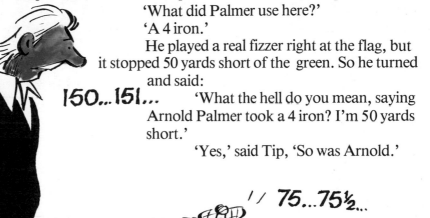

'What the hell do you mean, saying Arnold Palmer took a 4 iron? I'm 50 yards short.'

'Yes,' said Tip, 'So was Arnold.'

Golfing Greats

Tommy Bolt and Eric Brown, American and Scottish respectively, were two vitriolic characters. In the 1957 Ryder Cup match they were both missing about 10 minutes before their starting time. Someone asked Jimmy Demaret if he knew where they were and he said: 'Oh, they're standing at 20 paces on the practice ground throwing clubs at each other.'

Tommy Bolt was very self-conscious about his age. Once, when he was rather nearer 40 than 30, he was alarmed to see in the *Los Angeles Times* that he had been quoted as saying he was 49 years old. Eventually he was able to confront the miserable columnist and said to him:

'You son-of-a-bitch. What do you mean saying I'm 49. You know I'm 39.'

The journalist was flustered and could only reply:

'Yes, Tom. I know. It was just a typographical error.'

'Typographical error, my ass,' said Tom. 'It was a perfect four and a perfect nine.'

BOLT!

Tom was a very elegant man but also quite basic, and when they started bringing in new rules for the PGA tour in America he was rebellious. The authorities at that time also began fining people for all sorts of misdemeanours. Tom was once fined $25 for breaking wind on the first tee.

When tackled about that, he complained:

'Hell, they're taking all the colour out of the game.'

He dismissed some of the great players of the day by calling them 'flippy- wristed college kids'. Bolt was renowned for throwing clubs, and he also criticized the 'flippy-wristed college kids' for not being able to throw clubs properly. According to him, they always threw the club in such a way that they had to walk backwards rather than forwards to pick it up. He once suggested that he might open a school for club-throwers so players could get their clubs going in the right direction and at the right angle so that the club was not damaged.

Bolt was also the first player to be fined for practising before a tournament with more than one ball.

BOLTED!

IF THOSE PARACHUTES DONT
OPEN SOON MAYBE THEY WILL
GET HERE FIRST!

This restriction was brought in some years ago to save courses for tournament play. Until then it was fairly common for professionals going round a course to play a few extra shots from various places. This would make for a crop of divots, and more pitch marks on the greens.

The powers-that-be wanted to eliminate the extra balls, so they instituted a fine of $25 a shot. One day, soon after, Bolt was seen hitting an extra ball at one of the holes, so an official rushed out and said:

'Tom, that's a $25 fine.'

Tom reached in his pocket, pulled out a roll of notes, gave the official $100 and said:

'Keep the change. I may hit three more.'

Sam Snead, who still manages to play superb golf even though he's getting on for 70, has some great lines. On one occasion he was asked what he thought of a course, and he offered the view that the fairways were so narrow they had had to walk down them in single file. At another course he said the greens were so fast that he could only putt by holding the putter over the ball and hitting it with the shadow.

Most golfers tire occasionally of being asked the same old questions by reporters at tournament after tournament. One reporter caught Sam Snead on such a day.

'How did you find the greens, Mr Snead?' he asked.

'Sheet!' replied Sam. 'I just walked down the fairway and there they were.'

Much has been written about Ben Hogan over the years. He was almost a recluse and was supposed to have built a $150,000 house in Fort Worth, Texas, which had only one bedroom. The great wag Jimmy Demaret remarked:

'Well, Ben doesn't like entertaining people.'

He followed it up by saying that Ben was like the man who enjoyed porno films, but always ran them backwards because he liked to see people putting on their clothes and leaving.

I was practising with Julius Borus at the Master's Tournament in Augusta, Georgia when one of those executive jets boomed overhead with 'AP' in large letters on the tail. Julius said:

'Well, there's Arnold Palmer arriving.'

Half a hole later a similar executive jet boomed overhead with 'JN' on its tail. Julius said:

'There's Nicklaus.'

Ten minutes later a couple of old biplanes chugged by, at which Julius just looked up and said:

'My God, there's a sign of the times. You would have thought the caddies would have got here first.'

Clubhouse Tales

olf pros are sometimes accused of not having much sense of humour. A completely untrue story of four pros – myself, Dai Rees, Christy O'Connor and Eric Brown – has us playing an exhibition match in Aberdeen at the time of a blow-out at one of the oil rigs. We were sitting in the Station Hotel in Aberdeen having a drink. I looked up and saw a group of characters in stetsons and cowboy boots at the bar, and said to the assembled company:

'That's Red Adair.'

'Och, no,' said Eric Brown, 'that's no' Red Adair for Christ's sake.' I said, 'I think it *is* Red Adair.'

'No, I'll go and ask him,' said Eric. So he went over. 'Is that right you are Red Adair?'

'Yeah, yeah, boy, I sure am.'

'Well,' said Eric, 'I want to shake your hand. You are doing a great job, you're saving our oil before those sassanachs manage to take it all. You are going to have a drink with me.'

Adair thanked him very much and had a large bourbon. Eric returned to the table.

'You're quite right. That's Red Adair.'

'No, no, no,' said Dai Rees, 'I'm sure it's not Red Adair.'

'Go and ask him.'

So Dai went up.

'Now then boyo – nice to see you up yere. You can tell I'm not from these parts, you see, look you, but Eric Brown and I are golf pros – a bit long now in the tooth but he tells me that you are this great man who comes and puts out oil fires.'

'Yeah, indeed boy, I sure am. I reckon I've done a pretty good job here.'

'Well, it's not often we buy drinks you know, but I would like to buy you one as I think we in Wales might be a bit short of oil, we have plenty of coal but not much oil. You had better have something with me.' So Adair had another little taste of the bourbon. Dai came back, and I said:

'Was I right?'

'Yes you were right.'

Christy O'Connor quietly said, 'No no lads. I am quite sure it's not Red Adair at all.'

I said, 'Eric's satisfied it is. I know, and so does Dai, so why don't you go and ask?'

So Christy goes over.

> # Trevino, after hitting an unsatisfactory tee-shot:
> ## 'I knew I was swinging bad, but I had *such* a good grip.'

'Excuse me, sorr, I'm sorry to be interrupting you but they tell me you are this great man Red Adair.'

Red by this time was getting quite flushed with the bourbon and quite pleased with all the adulation.

'Yeah, you're quite right boy. I sure am Red Adair. What do you want to know?'

Christy leant over the table and said, in that light soft brogue:

'Tell me, what twas it really like dancing with Ginger Rogers?'

FRED ASTAIRE?
GET OFF, ITS
FREDDIE STARR!

The Crofter's Dream

Richard Dimbleby, so the story goes, was doing a series up in the Outer Hebrides and he came to a row of crofters' cottages. The cottages were beautifully maintained except for one in the middle which was very tatty. The garden was completely overgrown, the paint was peeling off the door and empty bottles of beer and Scotch littered the place. Just outside the door an elderly character was rocking to and fro. Richard Dimbleby thought there might be a story here so he walked up the path and said:

'Good morning, Sir, Richard Dimbleby, *Down Your Way*. In the midst of austerity you seem to be living the good life. Would you like to talk to us about it?'

The old Scot lit his pipe, took a swig of Glenlivet (he seemed to have plenty of baccy and booze) and said:

'Aye, aye, I'm very lucky. I've got a daughter, Aggie, she's what you call a whore, she's in Glasgow and sends me fifty pounds a week. Aye, aye. She's a good lass, Aggie.'

WHAT! YOU ACTUALLY STOOD

The old boy took a swig of beer chased down with a drop of Scottish wine, lit his pipe and rocked to and fro.

'I've also got a boy, Jamie, who's an assistant golf pro in Edinburgh. Aye, he's a good boy, Jamie, he sends me fifteen shillings a week. Mon, I wish he were a whore too.'

A Warm Welcome for Arnold

Arnold Palmer and I went to a dinner once, and Arnold got up at the appropriate time and went to the Gents. When he came back he was absolutely soaking through from the waist down. I said:

'God, what happened?'

He said, 'Well, I was standing there having a pee and this guy came up, stood beside me, turned and just said, "Jesus Christ, it's Arnold Palmer".'

NEXT TO ARNOLD PALMER!

Relief all Round

One of the best lines from an after-dinner speech came from Harry Carpenter. He was with me at the Sunningdale Golf Club, and after the meal the MC said:

'Gentlemen, before we hear from Harry Carpenter, I think we will have a five-minute break so we can all relieve ourselves.'

When eventually they got back, Harry rose to his feet and uttered the immortal words:

'I always like to go to a dinner where the audience take the piss out of themselves before they start taking it out of me.'

Good Shot!

I remember sitting with my father in his shop at Ferndown on a quiet morning when the door burst open and a man came in, threw his arms up and said:

'Percy!'

My father looked over the top of his glasses and said:

'Good morning.'

The chap said, 'Percy, you don't remember me.'

My father, ever a polite man said:

'Now let me have a look.'

The chap whipped off his cap with a great flourish.

'Now do you know me?'

'Just give me another second,' said father, frantically trying to remember. Suddenly the chap whipped away his glasses as though all was now revealed.

My father said, 'No, I'm afraid I'll have to give up.'

The chap was slightly crestfallen.

'Do you remember the Ryder Cup matches at Southport and Ainsdale in 1929?'

'Yes, I do.'

'Do you remember your match with Gene Sarazen?'

'I certainly do,' said father.

'At the second hole you pulled your tee shot just to the left-hand side of the fairway. The ball was on the fairway in fact but you were standing about six or seven inches above it.'

'Yes, I do remember that,' said Dad.

I didn't know whether he did or not. His face betrayed nothing. The chap went remorselessly on:

'Well, you played the most marvellous shot from there and pitched just short of the green and ran up to about eight feet away.'

'Yes, yes,' said my father.

'Well, I was the fellow who shouted "Good shot".'

Blind Man's Bluff

Lee Trevino looked up before his tee-shot one day at Gleneagles during the Pro-Celebrity series, and then stopped proceedings while he told the crowd round the tee the story of two golfers who agreed, for a change, to go round the course using their imaginations in place of golf balls.

The first player teed off and reported that he was straight down the middle of the fairway, about 230 yards. The second man played his shot and his ball also went straight down the middle and stopped about four feet ahead of his opponent's ball. On they went round the course, each man winning the occasional hole. They arrived at the 18th with the scores even. They both played good drives and the first player hit a 4 iron dead on target. He looked towards the hole in astonishment, then suddenly cried:

'It's in! It's in!'

'Goddam, so it is,' replied his opponent. 'But you played the wrong ball.'

Swedish Capers

One of the most ridiculous clubhouse stories concerns two friends of mine: David Thomas, my business partner, and Hugh Lewis, who was then the professional at Altrincham Municipal Golf Club, just south of Manchester. They had gone over to play some golf in Sweden. David Thomas, always a big man, delighted in taking saunas whenever he had the opportunity. Hugh was less keen but Thomas talked him into going down to a sauna cabin some 200 yards from their hotel, which was beside a lake on the outskirts of Stockholm. It was winter, and the weather was cold, wet and miserable. They got in the sauna and it was marvellous. The temperature was up around 100° when suddenly Thomas announced:

'Come on, let's run down, jump in the lake and splash the water on, then come back in here. If we do that a couple of times we will feel really great.'

Hugh had to be persuaded, but eventually they both got up. Out they went and splashed about in the water. Now the temperature had gone from 100° to minus plenty. They ran out of the water back to the cabin. Unfortunately the door had swung to and clicked shut on a Yale-type lock, and so there they were on the outside unable to get in. Both men were big, about 17 stone, but vulnerable now, stark naked, and 200 yards from their brightly lit hotel. Dusk had come and gone and it was almost pitch dark. What to do, what to do? There was no way of getting in through the door. Thomas's language deteriorated as he put the blame on to Hugh, telling him that he must go up to the hotel and get a key.

'I can't go up like this,' protested Hugh, through chattering teeth.

They had a quick scour round and found a rubbish bin with a plastic liner. Both sets of teeth were now well and truly chattering – remember the temperature. They knocked the bottom out of the bag and Hugh managed to wriggle into it rather like a woman putting on a girdle. Just then David, who had gone round to the back of the sauna, discovered a small window which they might be able to prise open. He found a piece of metal lying on the beach, inserted it in the corner and gave a great heave. He broke the window open, but the opening was only about 18 inches wide.

Thomas made Hugh bend over, rather like they do in those circus acts where the acrobats form pyramids eight men high, and clambered up on his back. I must confess this conjures up a marvellous picture for me: two lily-white Britishers, 17 stone, stark naked, are playing what looks like a weird game of leap-frog in the dark outside a sauna cabin 200 yards from a very swish hotel in Sweden. David then went headfirst at a window that wasn't designed to take anyone even half his size. Believe it or not, he got in.

Once in, he took another few minutes to open the door, just to teach Hugh a lesson. Hugh by this time, on his own admission, was so cold that he felt he could have joined the WRAF, or gone to a fancy dress party as a beach ball that had been blown up and had the teat pushed in. But that's another story.

Seven Ages of a Golfer

4 – 18 Every drive is smashed into the wild blue yonder. Putts go in from all over the green. 500-yard holes are reduced to a drive and a pitch. You go to bed at 10.00 or 10.30, get up at 6.30 for 100 practice balls before shooting off to college. As soon as you are old enough, you are allowed to borrow mum's little runabout car. For some years now, you have known that ladies were different shapes from boys. Now you have a chance to do something about it.

19 – 25 Smoking and drinking have made their inroads on the time that used to be devoted exclusively to golf, but every drive is still very much a boomer. Irons rule the pin, putting is still a mere formality. You buy your own first car, a black TR-7. The permanent girlfriend is now in tow and you take her out wearing your leather beer- drinking waistcoat, and prop yourself at the end of the bar. You hold the beer mug with the thumb through the handle and gaze at your love being chatted up at the end of the bar without a care in the world – having just won Saturday's medal.

26 – 30 You've gone and got married. Sex rears its ugly head in all legality. A baby in the first year. The sporty car has to go and is replaced by a rather staid two-year-old Cortina which has seen better days. You play golf only once a week but you still hit them quite well. The handicap has now gone up 3 to 8 and is slipping all the time. Putting is getting a little bit more difficult. Chip shots are the ones that are giving you the most problems. *Par Golf* magazine has been replaced by *Club International, Men Only* and *Playboy*. Your wife's folks hate golf and you begin to feel a touch, with the emergence of the second baby, that marriage might not be quite for you.

31 – 40 Two kids and a divorce. You were caught with that certain lady member at a far-off golf club, having told the wife you were going to play golf with the chairman of your company. What a tragedy to be found 75 miles away in the opposite direction. Disgrace, disgrace. You resign from the club. All the golfing gear is deposited in the attic. The car is sold, she takes the house, the kids, the cash and even that damn practice net. For you it's back to the bus and half pints of beer.

41 – 50 A revival – glory be. She remarries, against all the odds. What bliss. Once more you can think about the wonders of the game of golf. You recover the golf clubs. To hell with it. Let's have a new set. Dust off the old regime, on with the new. You join a club, buy a small BMW, start ogling the other members' wives and keep asking that pretty barmaid for another cold Löwenbräu from the very back of the cold shelf just to get a glimpse of her thighs. With lessons from the ageing golf pro it all starts to come back. Your first handicap is 14. The drive's not quite so far but the irons are still crisp. The putting is a little shaky but you can still hole out reasonably well. You think it even seems to have improved. You are sure you can make it. A four-time medal winner in your first year back at 'the game'.

51 – 65 Golf not too good. The large gin-and-mixeds are beginning to take their toll. Any drive over 175 yards is considered a gem. Any par 4 reached in 2 brings tears of joy to the eyes. Any hole three-putted is worth a loud whoopee. All the ladies at the golf club know your ploys and will have nothing to do with you. Even that spectacularly magnificent statuesque barmaid has left to get married. The woman you hoped to settle down with turned out to be just as much a soldier of fortune as you. Your clubs need regripping, indeed you could do with a new set. Gin has gone up again, you have a touch of piles, dandruff, and have developed a dreadful twitch on the green.

Over 65 Hair nearly all gone. Piles still troublesome. Any drive that gets off the end of the tee is considered good. No one rushes to play golf with you any more. You are even too bad for that 24 handicap. Any iron shot that gets into the air is a miracle. Chipping is hell and you have tried all the putting tips to try and stop the dreaded twitch. You are back to half pints of beer. You have lost all your cash in a mining-share disaster. The car has had it, the push bike's knackered but thank God you can still run a covetous eye over the caddymaster's wife. Cheers to golf!

The Golf Explosion

Japan and Sweden are two countries that you might not have thought of as being naturally golf-minded. Yet they have seen the two biggest booms in the recent expansion of the game.

The Swedish climate is not at all ideal for golf, but as a nation the Swedes are completely nutty about the game. In winter they play in indoor domes, and in proportion to their population they have more golf players than any other country in the world.

The Japanese story is all the more remarkable in that the tremendous growth there has been achieved in a country where only 17 per cent of the land is naturally usable for farming or building on. The rest consists mainly of mountain ranges.

I'm not sure what triggered it, but during the mid-late '50s the game simply took off there. In 1957 two Japanese, Ono and Nakamura, won the Canada Cup (which later became the World Cup). It was staged in Japan that year, and of course this must have helped the game.

Before we were aware of it, the Japanese were blasting the tops off mountains and bulldozing acres of rock. They crushed the rock almost to powder, and this became the topsoil of the new golf courses. On some of the steeper courses poles project from the sides of the mountains with netting stretched across them. If you go off the fairway, the ball runs into one of these nets, rather like waste draining into the scuppers of a ship. The caddy swarms down into the net and the ball (a very expensive item in Japan) is saved at the cost of a penalty stroke.

The caddies I saw there were nearly all women: tiny and of all ages, dressed in smart blue or red uniforms with strange-shaped hats and big scarves and a vizor sticking out in front so that you could hardly see their faces. Round their necks they carried little bags with a mixture of sand and seed. Every time you took a divot, they pulled out a little trowel and meticulously filled in the crater you had made, patting the surface down until it was perfectly flat again.

Recently I learned that the Mitsubishi company had built its own golf course. Membership costs £30,000,

Trevino, on hearing from his opponent that he would prefer not to talk: 'That's OK. You don't have to talk. Just listen.'

and a round of golf is about £80 a go. The green fee itself is about £18, and the rest is made up from local taxes.

Golf is an enormous perk in Japan. A tremendous amount of business is done at golf clubs, and it's one of the big signs that a man has been singled out for promotion if he graduates beyond the company car, and the Diners Club card for entertaining, to receiving golf lessons, and eventually joins the golf club.

It is reckoned, however, that about 70 per cent of Japanese golfers will never get on a golf course – in Japan. There just aren't enough courses. So they fly to Hong Kong or Taiwan for a golfing tour, or become driving-range experts.

With a full bag of kit, looking like Jack Nicklaus – well, a bit shorter – they go off to a driving range. There is a famous one that has three tiers, and room on each level for about 30 golfers. They only hit the ball 40 yards down the range, which looks like a large cage. They whack off about 50 balls and go home. It's a funny way to play golf – but the gear is magnificent.

WATCH BALL, PREASE!

A Golfing Fairytale

n 1964 a fellow-professional called Bert Williamson wrote a piece entitled *The Western Open*. To the best of my knowledge it has never appeared in print, but it is a good story which has been modified over the years. Here is the original. (I don't think you will have to be much of a golfing detective to discover the real names involved.) It was late on Monday evening when, from all different directions, they moved quietly and singularly into the old grey town of St Andrews. Each was a killer in his own right, each was a top class artist at his job. All had big reputations, all were individualists with their own personalities, but all were held together by a common cause, ramrodded by the mastermind of Mick McCormick who had brought them together once again for their annual raid on the local bank.

...'THUMBS POINTIN' DOWN THE SHAFT AND BREAK YOUR

McCormick arrived first and proceeded to make his headquarters at the Old Eagle Hotel, some miles out of town, from where he kept the one-man telegraph office tapping away with innumerable messages deep into the night. His college-boy face with heavy-lidded pale blue piercing eyes showed no sign of lack of sleep although he had spent the whole of the previous night travelling. Those eyes missed nothing and appeared as tireless as the man himself. Unlike those who joined him in this quest he was dressed in city clothes and was unarmed. Only his saddle-bags gave any indication of his calling. They apparently held nothing but legal documents but appeared very capable of carrying a vast amount of loot.

He was shortly followed by Gary 'The Kid' Plier, who still looked no more than 18 years of age and was dressed all in black with black gloves and an ornate belt. With pursed lips and deadpan face he hurriedly made his way behind what were the old railway sheds, away from the prying eyes of the local inhabitants, and proceeded to practise some pretty fancy shooting. His years as a top gunman were beginning to take their toll. Behind the young sun-tanned face were the eyes of an old man. It was already being said that he might retire to his ranch after this final raid.

Sitting alone with a glass of milk, 'The Kid' was joined later in a nearby saloon by the man many said was destined to replace him at the top. It was Big Nick Jacklaus, alias 'The Bear'. He dwarfed 'The Kid'. He greeted him with a knuckle-crushing handshake. His enormous strength was obvious to all who saw him but his rather slow gait was deceptive and belied his very delicate footwork when he went into action. His open, well-scrubbed, choir-boy, almost beardless face, topped by short-cropped golden hair, served only to mask his ruthless purpose. His pale eyes looked out innocently and greedily from beneath sandy eyelashes onto a world that owed him a living.

Champagne Tony Lima, sometimes called 'The Bean', kept well away from the hotels, saloons and gambling joints, well away from the rest of the gang. Together with an old buddy he stayed at the house of a widow-woman. Having just added five notches to his guns in as many weeks, he kept under cover, very much aware of the part he was expected to play. He'd even got religion and was known to spend much time on his knees conversing with the Good Lord. An unknown fighter only a few months before, he was now an up-and-comer and he knew it. The strain already showed on his face. He had that disconcerting habit of looking not straight at you but at a point somewhere behind you, as if searching for a lost friend in the crowd.

Lefty was the last to arrive, unnoticed. He was as inconspicuous as a bank clerk, which is understandable as that was once his job. Anyone less like a desperado would be hard to imagine. He looked even thinner than usual, his pallid face more drawn, but the old skill was still there and the killer instinct still within him. As usual he spent the night playing two-handed poker. Emotionless, his face was expressionless, his hands were quite nerveless; he remained silent but for an occasional grunt. The only member not to arrive was perhaps the greatest of them all: King Arney. Rumour had it that he was away forming his own private army to attack Columbus, Ohio. He was a true professional, the light of victory forever shining in his eyes. How they would fare without his great push and swashbuckling enthusiasm, time alone would tell.

The gang was well-organized and spent the next two days working out its final plan of attack. They augmented their strength by co-opting three or four well-known small-time henchmen from the South who knew their way around. These included Pam, Little Jack, Manchester Charlie, Chingi, and local boy Tip Anderson who had twice acted as sidekick to King Arney on his previous successful raids on Birkdale and Troon.

An electrifying air of expectancy, hard to define, pervaded the town on Tuesday night – the kind of atmosphere which always exists when it is known that a large sum of gold has been deposited in the strong-room of the bank. Even though such great fighters as Hunt, Alliss, Thomas and many others had been deputized to ensure its safety, this did not prevent the whole township staying up until the early hours of Wednesday morning.

Soon after dawn, helped by the hurricane which drove most people including the deputies to seek shelter indoors, everything went exactly according to plan. With ruthless, machine-like efficiency Lima snatched the lion's share and came away unscathed. Big Nick, although he took a slight mauling early on, recovered and took most of what was left. The deputies were left sprawling flat-footed and only Ben Hunt was able to salvage some 2,000 dollars from the wreck. Later, tired but triumphant, the gang slipped away with something like 500,000 dollars.

Champagne Tony, out of sheer bravado or in order to add to the legend that was fast surrounding his name, left sufficient money at the bar of the local hostelry so that the gentlemen of the press gathered there could drink champagne, and possibly by doing so write more luridly of his exploits. On Saturday, still stunned and dumbfounded at the cool audacity of the raiders, the old town of St Andrews quietly resumed its humdrum existence.

Municipal Deeds

There are three types of golf club in Britain – private, semi-private, and municipal. And the easiest to play on is the latter. The fact that you don't have to be a member, just turn up at the right time and hope to get on, has made the municipal course the setting for a fund of tyro-ignoramus stories, many of which, I am assured, are true.

Hedley Muscroft, who is the professional at the municipal course at Roundhay, tells the story of two chaps who turned up one day straight from work. One of them had his own clubs, paid his green fee, and explained that his mate also wanted to play and would like to hire some clubs.

Hedley said, 'Fine. Left or right-handed?'

The chap replied, 'I don't know yet. I've not played before. Give us a few of both.'

The Turf Garden

Hugh Lewis of Altrincham had a regular who played with a smallish bag with a long zip pocket down the side. Every time the chap came off the course this pocket was bulging with some strange substance. Hugh was mystified. He couldn't think what could be in there. No one had complained that anything was missing. In the end he couldn't contain himself and went over to the chap, who happened to have bought the bag off him a few weeks before, and tactfully said:

'You seem to be forcing a lot of stuff into that pocket. It doesn't to do the zip any good, you know.'

The chap didn't volunteer much, so Hugh felt compelled to press the point and asked him straight out what on earth he'd got in there. The chap opened the zip, and Hugh saw that the pocket was crammed full with big divots.

'What the hell are you doing with these?' he asked.

'Oh,' said the chap, 'I'm taking them home. I always put my

SPOILS THE GARDEN BUT IT WAS PART OF THE DIVOT!

PRO's SHOP

own back,' he went on. 'But these are ones that people haven't put back and they're lying out on the fairway. I've got this little garden at home and I'm making a lawn. I take these nice bits of turf home when they're damp and relay them. I get about a square yard every time I come up.'

'Well,' said Lewis, who was still flabbergasted, 'the next time Arnold Palmer comes over you ought to follow him. You should be able to get enough divots to returf the whole of your garden!'

The No. 7 Putter

John Stirling, the professional at Meyrick Park, Bournemouth, used to take evening classes. He'd give an hour's tuition in a church hall using plastic Airflow balls and a batch of No. 7 irons which he'd take down there in a golf bag. One winter's evening, after his class, he decided to take the clubs directly back to the shop. It was his day off the next day, so he took the bag, which contained 21 No. 7 irons, returned to the club, opened the door of his shop and pushed the bag round inside the door.

Next day he was at home pottering about when he realized that he had left his cheque-book on his desk. He went back to the club where his young assistant was looking after everything.

'How's it going?' asked John.

'Oh, very well, Mr Stirling,' answered his assistant. 'I've let out 22 hire sets today.'

'That's funny,' said John, 'we've only got 21 sets for hire.'

'Well, I've let out 22 sets,' said the assistant, showing John the page in the book where the clubs had been logged.

'That can't be right,' said John.

'Yes,' claimed the assistant. 'The clubs were all in the usual place ... oh, and someone said there was another set behind the door.'

At that moment a man came in carrying the bag with the 21 No. 7 irons. John, who had a great sense of humour, decided not to wait to be blown to pieces by the unfortunate golfer, who was bound to give him the most terrible rocket. Instead, he got his six eggs in first and said:

'Ah. Did you enjoy your game?'

'Oh, yes,' said the man. 'I've been playing for about six months now and that's the best sets of clubs I've ever had. But, next time, you might put me in one of those flat ones. On the greens it got a bit tricky.'

The Missus Came Too

Here is another Hugh Lewis story from Altrincham, where the 8th green was just by his shop window. One day he was in the shop, when somebody said:

'Hugh! Quick! Look out there.'

Hugh looked out. There on the green was a fellow lining up a six or seven-foot putt from all angles. Near him, in the middle of the green, stood a very attractive woman in high-heeled boots with a huge Silver Cross pram which she was jiggling up

and down, presumably to keep the occupant happy.

'Jesus,' said Hugh, and rushed out. He went up to the chap and started to reason with him. Keeping his back to the woman, and speaking as quietly as possible, he said:

'We really can't have this. I mean, it's not as if she's going round the edge of the green, she's right in the middle, in stiletto heels and with that great pram.'

'I know, I know, for God's sake,' replied the golfer, a desperate look on his face. 'I know it's difficult. But she won't let me out of the house unless she comes with me. So if she doesn't come, I don't get a game of golf at all.'

Hugh didn't know what to say. He felt genuinely sorry for the chap. As he turned away, he looked once more at the pram and noticed that, instead of a bag, the chap was laying his half-dozen clubs across the handles. Underneath was a basket with three or four golf balls and some golf tees. In a moment of lunatic inspiration, Hugh wondered if there wasn't room on the golfing market for a special pram on which you could rest your clubs and other golfing gear. Sanity, alas, returned and he never did anything about it, turning a blind eye to the pram and the high-heeled boots. Well, nearly a blind eye to the boots!

Running Repairs

On another occasion a customer came up to Hugh in his shop and asked him if he had an upholstery tack. Hugh said he didn't, but could offer a little nail of the kind then used for tacking leather grips to hickory-shafted putters.

The customer thanked him and asked if he could also borrow the vice on Hugh's workbench for a moment. Oh, and a hammer.

'Certainly,' said Hugh.

The customer then pulled from his pocket a golf ball with a huge cut in it. He inserted the ball in the vice, pushed the cover of the ball back in, then used the hammer to tap the nail into the side of the ball… and went out to play!

Blind Hole

When a blind hole is played, a large marker pole may be installed to show the way. Novice golfers have been known to go up to such poles, and solemnly lift them out of the ground – an action not unlike raising the caber.

Next, they force their ball through the two-foot-high grass surrounding the hole that they have just bared, and are surprised to find that the hole is three or four feet deep. Some are never able to recover their ball, even by lying flat on the ground with their whole arm jammed down the hole.

'Bloody funny golf course,' they say. And so it must seem.

Woman's Lot

The position of women in golf has been revolutionized since my playing days. With superstars like Nancy Lopez picking up huge prize money on the international circuit, it's a far cry from the early '50s, when woman's awareness of golf was more readily represented by a letter which arrived at Wentworth just before the Ryder Cup matches of 1953. In it the lady writer informed the secretary that her husband would very much like to come along to the Ryder Cup and she would be glad if he would send details. As a postscript she added: 'He wishes to watch, not participate.' There is still a general tendency for golf clubs to be condescending towards women members. There are many exceptions to this, such as you find at Formby in Lancashire, where there is a separate Ladies' Club alongside the men's, and the men may be invited to go and play on the ladies' course. That's good. I approve of that kind of separate development, without being a devotee of sexual apartheid in golf.

Many men like to relax in predominantly male surroundings, and circumstances usually decree that they must do this at weekends. This in turn tends to reinforce the male-held view that women should not play golf at weekends but stick to the weekdays when, it is assumed, they are free to play at least until the children come home from school.

For some, wife evasion is undoubtedly the name of the game, and obviously he can't evade her properly if she can easily get at him. 'We must do things together, dear. For the family's sake.' Such words have made more than a few husbands' toes curl up in rage and frustration as she reaches for her set of clubs.

Whatever the various women's movements may have achieved, the fact remains that a lot of men still like the idea of shutting themselves away and recalling the days before male chauvinist pigs were invented. Days when two visitors, husband and wife, arrived at the Royal St George's Club at Sandwich. As they were walking towards the clubhouse, they passed a man just leaving.

'Excuse me,' said the husband to the departing member. 'Are ladies allowed in the club?'

'Not sure about women,' came the reply. 'I know dogs are!'

Trevino's doctor: 'You know, Lee, jogging could add years to your life.'
Trevino: 'Oh I know that. I'm feeling ten years older already.'

On The Circuit

Going to the United States as a lad presented me with one or two communications problems. Sir Winston Churchill described Britain and the US as 'countries divided by a common tongue', and I know what he meant! In 1954 I was booking into a hotel in Los Angeles. While filling in the register, I realized that I had not left space for a proper forwarding address. Fortunately I was writing in pencil, so I asked the busty, rather attractive girl behind the desk:

'Could I have a rubber, please?'

She looked startled and asked me to repeat what I had said.

'A rubber please.'

'Just hold on one moment, please.'

She disappeared. I was leaning against the desk when suddenly the biggest man I had ever seen in my life emerged from behind the desk and came right up to me.

'What's your problem, buddy?' he asked.

'There's no problem,' I said, gesturing towards the register. 'I just want a rubber.'

'Jesus,' said the man, 'you mean an eraser. A rubber is a thing of an entirely different nature.'

On another occasion I was staying with a very hospitable American family. The next morning I wanted to go out on the golf course early, about 6.30, and the daughter of the house decided she'd like to get up and walk round with me.

FREEZE!

'All right,' I said brightly. 'I'll come and knock you up in the morning.'

Their eyes bulged in horror. As I now know, knocking-up is an activity 'of an entirely different nature.'

The Great Escape

I am perpetually fascinated by the ingenuity and effort that American commentators and TV people put into getting away at the end of golf tournaments and back to base in the shortest possible time.

I have been on two of these operations – which they call 'Great Escapes' – and I know that the planning that goes into them is amazing – an art, or a sport, in itself – and very funny when you consider all the things that could go wrong. Their greatest dread in a major event is a tie. A play-off ruins everything.

One of these nerve-wracking jaunts began at Pinehurst, in North Carolina. There we were, and the nearest airport with a service to New York was at Raleigh, 300 miles away. Play finished at six o'clock. Our television set-up was in the middle of the golf course, which was in the middle of a pine forest. But the American escape veterans had found a dirt-track which came out at a gate on the edge of the forest. Suddenly I'm in a car being driven by a 20-year-old student called Sal Johnson. We hurtled along the dirt road with pine trees about four feet in circumference flashing past eight inches on either side of the car. While we snaked through the trees, the loose sand flying, I thought, what the hell am I doing this for? Zoom, zoom, zoom go the trees. We could so easily crash into one. What a way to go.

We arrive at the edge of the forest, to be met by two motorcycle policemen who will escort us round and through the outskirts of a town to a school, where a helicopter should be positioned and ready. The policemen are very good. All the roundabouts are held up until we go by, the sirens are howling, lights flash, and we roar up to the school and into the helicopter.

The helicopter takes us to a small airfield about 30 miles away. There the escapers had arranged for a small plane, an eight-seater, to take us to Raleigh. And so it did. We got to Raleigh just in time. That is to say, the authorities had been alerted and were waiting for us. (Perhaps it is only fair to admit a slight advantage here, but in the United States the television companies carry enormous weight. If you ring up and say: 'I'm from ABC Television, snap, snap, snap,' and wave an invisible arm or two at them, it has tremendous impact.)

So far so good. As we get off the plane at Raleigh, another car is waiting to switch us at lightning speed from the light airplane side of the field to the public transport area. Here we are, brakes bite, four doors fly open and up the ladders we go. The plane leaves, and shortly we are in a holding pattern over New York. It's all right for the Americans, most of them live in New York, but I'm trying to get the 10 o'clock British Airways flight from New York

THEY'VE EITHER DISCOVERED OUR TUNNEL OR IT'S A TIE!

to London. I'm looking at the timetable, and now the excitement is really building. I could do it, I say to myself. Four hours ago, I was 1,500 miles away in the middle of a golf course in the middle of a pine forest. And now, here I am, I really could *just* make that plane to London.

At last we land, but at La Guardia, and I've got to get to JFK. It's Sunday night. The traffic's coming in from the beaches. Will I do it? It's 9.25. I rush up to the ABC limousine, and there's this chap with the half-chewed cigar. We set off, he driving with laconic skill, one elbow out the window, darting through the traffic. Kennedy Airport looms up. Rush in, sweating, eight pounds lighter in weight, heart leaping, a wreck. But they've been alerted, that's the thing. They've been told there's a late passenger for the London flight. I get up to the desk. A sweet girl there says:

'Oh, Mr Alliss. We've been expecting you. But we thought you'd be much later than this.'

How much later can you be, I thought. It's only minutes to take-off. They stamp my ticket, and I go through. Everyone is still in the departure lounge. I sit down. I'm still panting, beginning to reminisce about how I made it, feeling quite smug. Suddenly there's an announcement:

'British Airways regret to inform passengers that there's a 90-minute delay on this flight to London.'

Collapse in a heap.

I should not close this piece without mentioning Chuck Howard. He is one of the very senior executives in sports presentation at ABC, and he has pulled off some of the greatest escapes of all time. These have included a helicopter landing on top of a 30-storey building, a man on the ground floor holding the lift doors open while he waits for the police-escorted limo to arrive with Chuck in it. Up, up and away they go. The planning that Howard and others put in on these Great Escapes is quite staggering – and fun. Some of his escapes from golf tournaments would, I'm sure, make far better viewing than the tournaments themselves.

Henry and the Licence

The sayings and doings of Henry Longhurst are indispensable to golfing legend. I have noted down just a few here, and am grateful to Phil Pilley for letting me in on some that I hadn't heard. Phil Pilley was a BBC producer in the late '60s and early '70s and was responsible for many of the big golf programmes of that era before joining the Mark McCormack organization. In the course of those years Phil had ample opportunity to observe Henry Longhurst in his natural habitats, and travelled around with him a great deal. The first of the Pilley stories concerns Henry and certain dealings he had with the police.

Henry, although very keen on law and order, was not a great man in many ways for Authority. He didn't like paying licences. Licences for the dog, car, television, etc., etc. He usually managed to pay for his car licence, but about two months after time. Like his running battles with the Income Tax Authorities, this became something of a standing joke.

One day Henry arrived back at The Windmills, his house set high on a hill overlooking Hurstpierpoint in Sussex, to be met by the chap who cultivated his garden under a special crop-sharing arrangement.

'Mr Longhurst, the police have been.'

'Oh,' said Henry. 'What did they want?'

'A licence, I think. He said it was about some licence or other.'

'Ah,' said Henry, rather non-committally. He moved into the safety of The Windmills and poured himself a large Beefeater and soda. He sat down and thought: what licence could this be? Dog licence? Car licence? Radio and television licence? Gun licence? He worked through all the things he could think of, then found from his co-gardener that the police would be back at noon the day after tomorrow.

Henry's main objection to buying licences was that they got you 'on the list'. If you never paid, rather on the principle of the Romany caravanners, you'd never get caught for anything. Henry must have known that it was too late for him to think of escape, but this didn't stop him objecting to forking out 'unnecessary' money on licences.

He ran through his papers and narrowed the out-of-date licences down to three: television, dog, and gun. Next day he busied himself and renewed all three licences. Now he was rather looking forward to the arrival of the policeman. He would let him have his say, even lead him along a bit, and then with a flourish produce all his new, up-to-date licences.

The following day the policeman arrived at twelve o'clock and Henry, full of glee and expectancy, answered the door.

'Mr Longhurst?'

'Yeees.'

'Little word, Sir, about the licence.'

'Oh yes, indeed. Come in.'

As he showed the policeman into his living room Henry was clutching the new licences behind his back. He poured the policeman a beer and settled him in a comfortable armchair. This was going to be good, he thought to himself.

'Now,' said Henry, 'What seems to be the trouble about this licence?'

He brought his hand from behind his back and placed the three envelopes on the table. He knew exactly which envelope contained which new licence. He would produce them one after another as the policeman referred to them.

'Well, Sir,' said the policeman, 'it's about Mrs Brown and the licence. You're the referee for her application for the licence at the Rose and Crown.'

If only there was some record of Henry's face at that moment. For he had fallen, and was 'on the list'. The dreaded list.

Early Call

Phil Pilley worked with Henry on a gruelling TV series called *The Best 18 Holes in Britain,* played by the 'Big Three' – Palmer, Player and Nicklaus. They were only available for a short time and so they had to work to a hectic schedule and rush all over the British Isles by plane, helicopter, car and train from one venue to the next. One Saturday found them at Blairgowrie in Perthshire, where during the day they played and filmed the 17th hole. Only one more day's filming remained, down at Gleneagles. That was not until the Monday, but Henry did not know this.

They had had a long hard slog that week, and were feeling pretty exhausted when they finished at Blairgowrie at about 5.30. The players made their way down to Gleneagles, and Phil and Henry stayed behind to have a Scotch or two, and reminisce about the week's work. The weather began to deteriorate and quickly conditions outside became dreadful. They decided to have just one more for the road. Suddenly Phil announced:

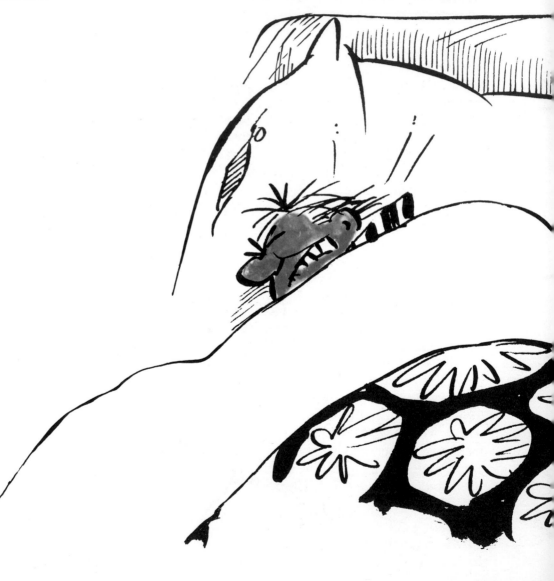

'Henry, tomorrow you've got a day off. No need to get up early. You're completely free until Monday.'

'Hmm, good,' Henry seemed to be thinking. Aloud he said, 'Well, perhaps just one more then.'

By the time they drove off for Gleneagles, Henry had had plenty and Phil had had enough. It was dark, they faced a strange road, and the rain was pelting down. Phil drove their borrowed car, and Henry got into the back, falling asleep almost immediately. Phil, hunched at the wheel, peered through the grimy windscreen at the wet, unlit road. The wipers ploughed back and forth. Twigs blew off trees. Suddenly the Great Man stirred.

GOOD MORNING, SIR.
THIS IS YOUR EARLY—
WHAT WAS **THAT?**

'Phil,' he said, 'I don't wish to disturb your driving, but I just wanted to check something with you. Are you quite sure that there's absolutely nothing happening tomorrow?'

Phil reassured him. 'Yes, Henry. No need to put in the 5 o'clock call. Tomorrow you're completely free.'

Henry grunted and went to sleep again. Ten minutes later Phil felt a tap-tap on the shoulder.

'Phil, I really don't want to go on about this, but I do want to get it absolutely clear. Are you really quite certain that there's nothing at all to be done on Sunday?'

'That's right, Henry,' replied Phil. 'Absolutely nothing. You're not required, in any shape or form, until Monday morning. So you can forget the early morning call.'

In the back of the car there was silence for a few seconds and then Henry came out with:

'Hmmm. It almost makes you want to book one, just so you can tell 'em to stuff it!'

The Public Speaker

Many of the famous American golfers held Henry in particular awe because, soon after the war, Henry had been a Member of Parliament – albeit for not very long. One day Phil Pilley found himself riding in the back of a car through the streets of West London with Henry and Arnold Palmer. They stopped at some traffic lights in Acton. Henry suddenly looked out of the window and said:

'You see that greengrocer's over there? That's where it all began for me, you know.'

'What was that, Henry?' asked Palmer.

'That,' said Henry, 'was my campaign office when I became Conservative MP for this area.'

'Really,' said Palmer, looking interested. He encouraged Henry to tell the story of how on election night the votes had been counted and how he had just squeezed in by a small majority. Great jubilation amongst all the helpers and friends. Eventually it was time for Henry to go out and meet the populace. He climbed up on some beer crates and took his place on the back of a wagon. Someone handed him a megaphone. Here Henry paused in his reminiscence to reflect on that glorious night.

'Well,' said Arnold Palmer, growing slightly impatient as the seconds passed. 'What happened? What happened?'

'Oh,' said Henry, 'I gave them some of my finest stuff. I felt I was going to change the course of the world, certainly the course of the Conservative Party. I gave them a really solid piece of rhetoric.'

'Ah,' pursued Palmer, 'and what did they say?'

'Well,' said Henry, rather sorrowfully, 'they all just murmured "Balls".'

Priorities

Henry Longhurst was a great believer in health farms. He used to go off for a week or two weeks and there, with not one drop to drink, he used to do a lot of writing while at the same time shedding what he saw as the equivalent of one or two sets of golf clubs, i.e. 14 or 28 pounds. It was after one of his stays at the health farm that Phil Pilley went down to see Henry at his house in Sussex.

It was a beautiful spring day in early May, and they were sitting outside having a glass of cooling something-or-other. Phil asked Henry:

'Do you really enjoy going to these health places? It seems a lot of money to pay to be starved. Can't you just stay at home and discipline yourself not to overdo it?'

'Oh no,' Henry said. 'That's very difficult. And anyway I enjoy the peace and quiet there. No telephones. I can just read the newspapers quietly. It's absolutely marvellous.'

'Oh,' said Phil, impressed. 'Perhaps I might try it one day.'

'Yes, you ought to,' said Longhurst. 'I come back after a couple of weeks and I feel marvellous. My tongue is clean, my eyes are bright. I sit here and think to myself, is there really nothing better to do but take the car out of the garage and go down into Hurstpierpoint and drink gin at the New Inn?'

Here Henry paused. 'And, of course, there never is.'

Fear of Flying

Neil Coles hates flying, and there is a story – a total fabrication – which has him going off on a private flight with myself, Sir Douglas Bader and Wing Commander Julius Bronowski, VC, DSO, etc., who was blind and had to tip-tap his way slowly up the plane while dear old Bader stomped around encouraging him.

Coles asked if we were really sure it would be all right.

'Oh yes,' replied the old Polish war ace. 'It'll be fine. But, look, if you're worried, I'll leave the curtains open so that you can see everything I do.'

Coles said, 'Yes, but you're blind.'

'Yes,' said Bronowski. 'But what happens is, Douglas takes me to the end of the runway, then I just throttle back and off we go.'

Coles said, 'But how do you know when to pull back and take off?'

The ageing ace replied, 'Well, I usually wait until I hear the client shout, "Jeeesus Christ!!"'

The Putting Yips

Henry Longhurst and I were agreed that there were two types of putting 'yip' – that involuntary and painful nervous twitch that most golfers know about and which was beautifully described by Angela Patmore in her book *Playing on their Nerves*. If you had a long slow backswing and then collapsed the left wrist at impact so that the ball floated away out to the right – rather in the style that I used to miss them – that shot was called a 'Semprini'. If you can recall Semprini sitting at the piano, in evening dress, reeling off tunes for 'old ones, loved ones, near ones, dear ones, neglected ones', with the hands flowing gently through, you may see a certain similarity.

Then there is the other type of putt that jerks away to the left, with the right hand overtaking the left at a tremendous rate. That was known as the 'Russ Conway' or the 'Winifred Attwell', in deference to their marvellous pounding cross-handed techniques.

Henry and I had a lot of fun over the years spotting the Semprinis and others with 'a touch of the Winnie Attwells'. Happy happy days.

Hide the Noddy

This was a game devised by one of my good friends, Hugh Lewis (whom we met earlier in the sauna episode and in 'Municipal Deeds'). He and I and one or two others, including David Thomas, my business partner, and a friend called Alan Gillies became involved in Lewis's dreadful creation. It centred on the Noddy, which was the operative word for a french letter. If, in the course of some gathering, the cry went up: 'Noddy hidden!' this meant that one of these dreaded articles had been hidden in a way likely to cause great embarrassment to the person who found it.

They became highly ingenious about finding hiding-places. If they went to stay somewhere for the weekend, they would stuff one into a sock. Next day, when the sock was due to go into the washing machine, a Noddy would fall to the floor in front of a puzzled wife. Behind the sun vizor in a motor car was another place – they got me with that. Well-known players about to embark on exhibition matches or tournaments, and looking full of self-importance, would pull the head-cover off their driver on the first tee, and the packet of three would drop out in full view of everyone. Some of the undignified scrambling about that ensued had to be seen to be believed.

In one master-stroke, while staying at a friend's house, they actually stretched one over the handle of their friend's wife's Hoover. Being transparent, it was there for several days before the poor wife noticed. There were great shrieks of delight, meanwhile, from the perpetrators as they imagined the wife – a rather prim lady – making innocent hand movements up and down the column of her carpet beater as she banished the dust with brisk but firm strokes.

These crude, rather schoolboyish pranks continued for some time and attracted a certain amount of fame. One day, after I had been 'Noddied' on the first tee at a tournament (it fell out of my glove), I decided I would try to get my own back.

There was to be a drinks party at Hugh Lewis's house, where I was staying at the time. Some hours before the party I got one of the ice trays out of the refrigerator, put my Noddy in one of the little compartments, filled the tray up with water, and slipped it into the back of the refrigerator. When the right moment came, I made sure that I got Hugh Lewis's next gin. I put three lumps of ice in, making sure that my loaded one was at the bottom, and covered all three with a generous slice of lemon. The glass was of the finest crystal, and when I had finished my preparations the result looked like a really solid, home-poured gin and tonic.

Hugh accepted it with a charming smile and carried on chatting away. I joined the group he was with, and watched with quiet satisfaction as the two upper cubes melted. Just as the third cube was on the point of disintegrating, and the offending article floated to the top, I managed to say gently to Hugh:

'Noddy hidden.'

Memory fails to recall who he was talking to at the time (not the vicar, alas), but I can remember that his embarrassment was acute. After that incident, we called 'Pax!' and no more Noddies were hidden.

Foreign Parts

For several years David Thomas, my old partner Pat Dawson and I have had a company called Golf Construction, and we have built many golf courses throughout the world. In our experience the discovery of oil, coupled with the fresh influx of Caucasians into those countries to develop the oilfields, has had a lot to do with the expansion of golf, bumping up the demand for new courses.

The oilmen arrive, and the companies wonder how to entertain them. So they build a clubhouse offering a bar, restaurant, tennis courts, squash and eventually, because the new workforce is going to be around for a few years, they put in a golf course.

In West Africa they didn't have grass greens, they had what they called 'Browns', made from a mixture of very fine earth and oil. The caddies carried a kind of dragmat, and after you'd finished on the putting surface they would tow the mat around and round to smooth it out for the people coming up behind. We studied the longitude, latitude and so on, and found that Nigeria had pretty much the same climate as Singapore. So we knew we could grow grass greens there – not immaculate ones, but they were generally successful.

While we were in Nigeria, we received a memorable letter from a Mr Nwankoo Okike about a site we were clearing on which his father had put a juju shrine. The funerary honours of the family had to be respected, and Mr Okike wrote as follows:

Trevino, on hearing that his opponent is twenty-seven years old:

'My Gaad! I've got socks older than you. And they are still in perfect working condition.'

Dear Sir,
With reference to the Juju shrine prepared by my father and kept at Ogbeano, Kalabari Beach, Oguta. I hereby write to inform you that the following things must be presented to me for sacrifice to the juju before it can be removed to my town: one goat, one he-sheep, one dog, three fowls, one Schnapps, one piece of white cloth, one head of tobacco.

All the above items must be ready at the spot before I could perform anything. Furthermore when this is removed to my home a house must be built to place it in. Transportation of the juju and feeding allowances must be included. This juju is prepared for the members of my family.

After the above I estimate my total charge to be 2,000 naira (£2,000). It is out of this estimated amount that after building its house at my home part of it will be used to buy one cow for the first sacrifice to it.

With the above explanations you should realise my charge to do it is not too much. On the day I come for removal you will give me labourers to assist me destroy the place. Thanks in anticipation.

Yours faithfully,
N Okike.

A certain amount of bargaining followed, and I am happy to recall that he settled in the end for a fiver, a box of golf balls and a leg of lamb.

Building golf courses out in Africa has its funny and its tedious sides. The graft that goes on is amazing. You can't even get your passport stamped unless you enclose the appropriate bank note. You can stand there all day long and the official will just ignore you. At the hotels you can produce sheaves of papers confirming your reservation, but until you come across with the necessary it's all 'No room, no room.' Until you know the game, it's a nightmare. As for getting paid or getting money out of the country, well!

Once, we were waiting for a cheque for £84,000 to come through from West Africa to the Manchester branch of Barclays Bank. We were assured that the money had been transferred from the country bank down to the capital. Two, then three weeks went by and we heard nothing. So my partner Pat Dawson got on a plane to Africa and went to see the manager of the bank. They started to do some detective work, and traced the payment to the in-tray of a junior clerk. The cheque had to be taken out of the tray, stamped, and put into another tray. The catch was, the clerk wouldn't do it until he had been given the equivalent of £5. He wanted his fiver, and he stuck out for it. Ah, the joys of big business!

On the lighter side, I remember a line of African workers near a course we were building. They were tilling the land with rather primitive implements. It was in the bush and some of these fellows hadn't got a stitch on. They were rather well hung and, working in line to a steady rhythm, the marriage equipment was waving from side to side, side to side – rather like a row of baby elephants' trunks. We had an American oilman and his wife with us. Suddenly she turned to her husband and said:

'Honey, you'll have to get me out of here soon, otherwise I'll start thinking you're de-formed!'

79

Celebrity Golf

The Pro-Celebrity series has played a huge part in converting golf into family entertainment. When the purist golfers tell me that they don't want to watch a lot of actors and comedians, they want to see Arnold Palmer and Jack Nicklaus playing Tony Jacklin and Gene Littler 24 hours a day, I try to point out that's not really the object of the exercise.

Our programmes have to be entertaining in such a way that they collect the fringe audience. Take a household of four or five people: only one of them plays golf, and there's only one TV set in the house. They are almost bound to be in for everlasting battles about what they watch. But, if in our golf programme we can offer Sean Connery, or Glen Campbell or Johnny Mathis taking part on one side, and Bobby Charlton or Ray Reardon or James Hunt on the other, plus the pro golfers, we're likely to get many more people interested. Even four out of the five in our imaginary family may be entirely happy. And the other one doesn't mind watching because he or she gets a tranquil 45 minutes looking at the lovely views.

We've certainly had a lot of fun doing the various competitions involving celebrities. The golf is sometimes a little bit variable, but again that's all part of the excitement – and the embarrassment in at least one case.

The Case of Mr X

We had one American film actor over, whom on reflection we had better call Mr X.

Anyway, he arrived at Gleneagles and it was automatically asumed that he played golf. He said his handicap was 24.

Trevino, on shaping to hit a delicate little chip shot:
'Just watch this one land . . . like a butterfly with sore feet.'

Well, never mind, we thought, he was here and everything would probably be OK.

He set off on the first hole, which was the 8th for that series, after which we went across to the 11th on the King's Course and then played our way in. On the tee he had about five air shots and then finally whistled one into the ferns which were about eight feet ahead. I got this voice in my ear – commentators have little ear-pieces with a battery on the back – which said:

'Scrub this hole. On to the next.'

Well, still there was no great panic around, and we got to the 11th. This time he had a swing at it. I must confess the swing did not look too bad but he caught it a bit low and it rattled into a bunker short of the green. The other three players were all safely on so Mr X got into the bunker. It really did look as though he was attempting to kill a snake. He was hacking and chopping away and his score was almost chanted in unison: '8, 9, 10...' On the 12th or 13th shot he suddenly caught the ball cleanly and it sailed over the green some 80 yards. The by now rather irate producer said:

'Cut this one as well. Cut, cut.'

On to the third hole. Mr X had another vicious swing at this with a wood and caught the ball on the toe end. The ball flew towards an unsuspecting chap who was just leaning forward to get a good view, resting his hands on the handle of his umbrella. There was a crack like a pistol shot and the poor man's thumb, which was shattered, came up like a balloon. A voice in my ear said:

'I don't think this is any good.'

I replied in some good old Anglo-Saxon words that it was a complete waste of time being out on the course. What this chap was doing here I really did not know and the sooner he returned to his native shores the better. Unfortunately it did not come out as politely as that, and my expletives boomed round the hospitality TV sets in the hotel. I must confess we had one or two rather red faces that night. Including mine!

The story that eventually emerged was that Mr X had been asked when he went to the Bel Air country club in Los Angeles whether he played golf, and he had said, truthfully:

'Yes.'

'Would you like to go to Gleneagles in Scotland to take part in a Pro-Celebrity golf match?'

'Yes.'

'Would you like to bring your wife, or daughter, or whoever?'

'Yes, that's very nice of you.'

'The invitation lasts a whole week.'

'Fine, I should be delighted to go.'

The only trouble was that Mr X was not asked, and did not offer the information that he had had only two or three golf lessons in his life. Still, at least it kept the producer on his toes.

The Sound of Mathis

When the great American singer Johnny Mathis was performing at the Wakefield Theatre Club, I went with Ronnie Sumrie, a great friend of mine, and our ladies to see the show, and the following day we had a game of golf at my own club, Moor Allerton.

We got to the 8th, which is a dreaded hole, uphill into the prevailing wind. It's really about 580 yards but plays about 8 miles. I managed to get a drive going forward about 220 yards. Ronnie, who has a rather short jerky backswing but does make beautifully cut slacks for his living, whizzed one with the heel of the club and scuttled up the fairway about 190 yards.

Mathis is a very enthusiastic golfer and in his younger days was a very fine hurdler and high-jumper. He hit his first one clean out of bounds.

'Give me another ball, caddy.'

Another new Titleist appeared, the paper torn off and the ball carefully placed on the tee. That sailed over the road, over the trees, never to be seen again.

'Another, please.'

Same procedure, but this time even further out.

'Another one.'

By this time the conversation was becoming very stilted indeed. The final one went up into the bushes on the right somewhere, and Ronnie and I moved forward. We did not notice that John had held back a bit, and suddenly this beautiful voice rang out singing the scale and ending on the highest note. We turned in amazement.

'Thank God I can still sing,' said Mathis.

Eric in the Sauna

Eric Sykes has travelled the world as a celebrity golfer, and many a far-off watering hole has had its fame increased among golf people for something that he said or did there. One Sykesism goes back to a holiday in Marbella, when Jimmy Tarbuck, Kenny Lynch, Sean Connery and many others were enjoying the then new-found golfing oasis on the Costa del Sol. Eric is very deaf and gets his leg pulled unmercifully. On this particular occasion several of the lads were in the club sauna, which had a large glass panel door through which the occupants could see whoever was approaching.

Looking through the panel, Jimmy Tarbuck observed Eric making his way towards the sauna with a towel wrapped around his waist. In an inspired moment he said to the assembled company:

'Whatever he says, don't answer. Pretend you haven't heard a word.'

Everyone agreed, and Eric entered the sauna.

'Good morning all, good morning, good morning.'

Not a word, Someone shuffled up to make room for Eric to set his towel down. He put his bottom on the bench and started looking around.

'Well I don't feel too bad considering. I must confess I had one or two brandies and a couple of big cigars last night.'

Still complete silence.

'How long are we going to stay in here? Are we going to play nine holes or eighteen before lunch, or what's happening?'

Not a word. By this time Eric had twigged something was up. He said nothing. Ten, fifteen minutes went by. The temperature in the sauna rose and the sweating went

on and on and on. Suddenly Sykes could stand it no more, and he looked up and said:
'Can anyone tell me what time this train gets into Calcutta?'

Eric in Africa

In 1979 Eric Sykes went to Kenya with a Variety Club outing for the Kenya Pro-Am.
He got the runs, and for a while was very poorly. His first outing when he did get better was to a famous Masai village where the natives made everything out of cow dung. The smell and the flies were terrible. Eric got out of the coach and, seeing a half-built hut, said:

'Pity I didn't get here a few days earlier. I could have helped them finish that one.'

Clubhouse Clangers

Golf, rather like cricket, has always been a game that has attracted characters, good writing, and strange, black humour. My first introduction to the so-called black humour of golf happened many years ago when my father was the professional of the Ferndown Golf Club, six or seven miles north of Bournemouth.

It was my father's habit to buy three morning newspapers. I had just left school and become his assistant, and it was our habit to make our way over to the pro shop at about a quarter to nine and sit in two big armchairs that he had brought from Germany some twenty years before, and read the news.

Ferndown in those days was not an 'early' golf club. I had waded through the *News Chronicle* and the *Daily Mail,* and was waiting to get to grips with the *Daily Mirror* when suddenly the secretary's door opened. The secretary at that time was a Welsh gentleman called Wyn Williams. He, together with a rather tall, gaunt young gentleman came down the steps, walked to the first tee, sort of sniffed the air, and began to look around. After ten or fifteen seconds or so we lost interest in them.

At that moment one of the great characters of the club entered the pro shop. His name was Joe Close. He was a retired dental surgeon and to me he was like a god – though some people mistook his direct approach for that of a golf club bore. He came in smoking his pipe, puffing great clouds of smoke in the air, grabbed a paper and started reading the news. With nothing to do I looked up and noticed that Mr Williams, the secretary, and

Trevino on ageing: 'Grey hair is great. Ask anyone who's bald.'

his guest had returned to the secretary's office. Joe continued to read his paper in silence.

The secretary's door opened again and out came the two men carrying a small square box about the size of a dozen golf balls. They walked quietly around the 18th green, stopping here and there to sprinkle white powder, seemingly in selected areas of the putting surface. (It should be said that Mr Williams had recently taken over from one J C Beard, an acknowledged expert in the art of bringing on perfect golfing greens. Mr Williams wished to follow Mr Beard's success and was forever trying new things. Joe, for one, did not always appreciate his efforts.)

Fifteen or twenty minutes later Joe announced that it was time for a hot Ribena, a cup of bovril or a half of beer. We all walked over to the clubhouse and there at the bar were Wyn Williams and this tall, rather gaunt young man.

DAMMIT! WHAT ARE THEY DOING TO THE GREENS THIS TIME?

Joe, with the force of a charging water buffalo, marched straight up to the bar and said:

'Well, what bloody muck are you putting on the greens now?'

There followed the loudest silence I have ever heard in my life.

'Er, Mr Close,' said Wyn Williams at last. 'May I introduce you to Mr Donaldson. His father wished to have his ashes scattered around the 18th green at Ferndown, and we have complied with his wishes.'

The Club Cat

Here is another black tale which animal-lovers may not thank me for, but Harry Weatman used to rejoice in telling it, and I pass it on mainly to ensure that it should not be forgotten.

A golf club somewhere in Surrey once had a young sandy-haired Scottish assistant who was on a very short fuse all the time. Very quick-tempered. He was out one day playing behind the club captain, and as usual was getting more and more impatient. Twice he drove early, and the captain was very put out to see the assistant's ball run past him as he was walking up the fairway.

The captain kept looking back darkly, but the assistant took little notice. Afterwards, he was called into the secretary's office.

The office was probably the finest room in the clubhouse. It had a large bow-window overlooking the 18th green, a wonderful collection of golfing books in shelves on the wall, a pile of golf magazines on a low mahogany table. In the air hung the gentle odour of pipe smoke. There were big leather armchairs by the fire and a mound of coal glowed orange and red in the grate. In front of the fire lay the club cat, a big old ginger puss snoozing away. It had just had a nice piece of boiled fish and was stretched out blissfully on the rug.

The old secretary did not shirk his duty and began giving the young man a fairly stiff wigging.

'This is not what we expect from you,' he was saying, 'the captain is most upset and you have also put me in a most awkward...'

Suddenly the assistant had had enough. He bent down, grabbed hold of the cat, with one jerk wrung its neck and tossed the still-twitching body among the papers and scorecards on the secretary's desk. He stormed from the room and was not seen again.

When the officials at the club had recovered from their shock, they decided they were well off without their young assistant. If he could do that to the club cat, while it lay drowsily digesting a delicious piece of turbot and thinking that all was well with the world... why, reasoned the club officials, he might soon be doing it to the lady captain.

'The most important distance in golf is the
six-inch space between the players' ears.'

Bobby Jones